LIVING WILL, LIVING WELL

living will,
LIVING WELL

reflections on preparing an advance directive

M. Dianne Godkin, RN PhD

UNIVERSITY OF ALBERTA PRESS

Published by

The University of Alberta Press
Ring House 2
Edmonton, Alberta, Canada T6G 2E1

Copyright © 2008

Library and Archives Canada Cataloguing in Publication

Godkin, M. Dianne, 1961-
 Living will, living well : reflections on preparing
an advance directive / M. Dianne Godkin.

Includes bibliographical references.
ISBN 978-0-88864-494-7

 1. Advance directives (Medical care). I. Title.

R726.2.G64 2008 362.17'5 C2008-900638-0

The University of Alberta Press is committed to protecting our natural environment.
As part of our efforts, this book is printed on Enviro Paper: it contains 100% post-
consumer recycled fibres and is acid- and chlorine-free.

The University of Alberta Press gratefully acknowledges the support received for its
publishing program from The Canada Council for the Arts. The University of Alberta
Press also gratefully acknowledges the financial support of the Government of Canada
through the Book Publishing Industry Development Program (BPIDP) and from the
Alberta Foundation for the Arts for its publishing activities.

Contents

Foreword vii

Acknowledgements ix

ENCOUNTERING DEATH AND DYING · INTRODUCTION 1
    Reflecting on an Uneasy Death
    Honouring Martha's Legacy
    Asking the Questions
    Defining the Terms
    Tracing the History
    Exploring the Benefits and Barriers
    Setting the Stage
    Introducing Alice

1 · PROTECTING SELF AND OTHERS 15
    Noticing Advance Directives
    Focussing on the Future
    Listening Attentively
    Desiring Comfort and Peace
    Experiencing the Death and Dying of a Loved One
    Controlling Technology
    Fostering Family Relationships
    Preserving One's Identity

2 · FACING ONE'S MORTALITY 43
    Meeting Death
    Interacting with Death
    Accepting Death
    Disappearing Death

Living Life
Sitting Quietly

3 · TALKING ABOUT DEATH 65
Conversing at the Dinner Table
Joking About Death
Widening the Discussion
Considering a Parent's Death
Imposing Limits on the Discussion
Talking to No One

4 · CHOOSING AN ALLY 81
Naming an Agent
Selecting the Best Agent
Trusting Your Agent

5 · GETTING IT DONE 95
Gathering Information
Personalizing the Data
Writing and Rewriting
Keeping It Simple
Following the Rules
Reflecting on the Process
Looking Toward the Future

CLOSING THOUGHTS · CONCLUSION 115
Reconsidering Expectations
Summarizing Key Findings
Messages for Healthcare Consumers
Specific Challenges for Healthcare Providers
Apprehending Death

Reference List 129

Appendices 137
Appendix A: Guiding Interview Questions
Appendix B: Sample Advance Directive
Appendix C: Legislative Guidelines
Appendix D: Educational Resources

Index 151

Foreword

As Dianne Godkin so sensitively and compellingly points out, there
is a significant need for everyone to think about what might await
them as their life's journey ends. This need stems in large part from
the advances in technology which are life-saving to many people,
prolonging their lives in a completely desirable way. However, the
same technology can be merely death-postponing to others and bring
them no acceptable benefit. *Living Will, Living Well* is designed to help
us think about these things while there is time, and when we are not
in "crisis mode"—and it succeeds in this chief aim in a compelling
and beautiful way.

My hope is that all the many readers who should be made aware
of this book will agree with this opinion, and act upon the resolve
which forms in their minds as they read it. They should take note
of the author's suggested steps as they form their opinions on these
important matters. These key factors include: protecting oneself and
others; facing one's mortality; choosing an ally or substitute decision-
maker; talking to loved ones; fostering patient–healthcare provider
relationships; and examining one's attitudes and beliefs about death
and learning to talk about them.

In *Living Will, Living Well*, Dianne Godkin follows the course of
"Alice"—a composite person whom she has generated from the actual
experience of 15 older persons. Alice attends a meeting in a church
basement, where she hears a lawyer speak on the topic of making
"advance directives." This technique is successfully used to draw
those 15 actual persons' views, opinions, difficulties, whims and
idiosyncrasies into a coherent story that embraces the author's five

themes: protecting self and others; facing one's mortality; talking about death; choosing an ally or decisions partner; and actually making the directive. The author interpolates Alice's narrative with discussion sections in which she draws not only on these research experiences, but also on her extensive reading of the published literature on this important subject. She then comments on factors which may deter persons from going on with initial resolve to make a personal treatment or proxy directive, such as the legal implications of the process, and the wording of legislation in Alberta and other provinces. Dianne Godkin manages to humanize the whole process, making it much easier for those wishing to make their wishes known in advance to discuss these matters with their families as well as with their "proxy decision-makers" and healthcare providers. She deplores the fact that the language of the legislation does not include enough emphasis on the importance of fostering our relationships and dependencies when it comes to such important decisions. Such advance directives, it is made clear, are only to be followed when the person has lost the capacity to make actual real-time decisions.

Whether a person thinks of death as a "great adventure," as does Alice, or as a sad and tragic end of their existence, decision-making at the end of life needs sound information about the medical possibilities and their probable outcomes. Enabling "comprehended choice" by those making advance directives requires full discussion with healthcare professionals—from several disciplines—in order to reach a good decision. This places a real obligation on those health professionals who may not have had these new perspectives as part of their training or outlook when they set out on their careers—that is, before the development of recent life-sustaining technologies.

This book is aimed at promoting "comprehended choice" in the matter of end-of-life advance decision-making. In my opinion, it succeeds.

I hope it will be widely read by many types of health professionals as well as by all those over 65 years of age, even when they are in good health, and that it leads them to making good decisions. This book is not only a valuable contribution to this area of healthcare, it also has philosophical beauty.

John B. Dossetor, OC, BM-BCh (Oxon), FRCPC, PhD
Emeritus Professor (Medicine & Bioethics), University of Alberta

Acknowledgements

The most precious gift we can offer others is our presence.
-*Thich Nhat Hanh*

When the opportunity to publish a book based on the findings of my dissertation research arose, I couldn't have been more excited. I have been accompanied by many individuals along this journey, and I would like to acknowledge the many gifts I have received from them.

A great supervisory committee from the University of Alberta including Dr. Vangie Bergum (Chair), Dr. Wendy Austin, Prof. Gerald Robertson, Dr. Marjorie Anderson, and Dr. Brenda Cameron nurtured my development as a scholar through their support and encouragement. My fellow graduate students with whom I spent many memorable hours engaging in lively debate were a source of inspiration and friendship.

Funding to support my doctoral education was gratefully received from the Canadian Institutes of Health Research (formerly the National Health and Research Development Program), the Alberta Heritage Foundation for Medical Research, the Canadian Nurses Foundation, the University of Alberta, the Faculty of Nursing (University of Alberta), and Mu Sigma Chapter of Sigma Theta Tau International Nursing Honour Society.

My parents, siblings, and many nieces and nephews have always been my strongest cheerleaders. I am thankful that they have always been there for me and that they keep reminding me of what is really important in life.

I would like to thank the University of Alberta Press for publishing this book, and in particular extend thanks to Leah-Ann Lymer for providing her editorial expertise.

Early in my career, I had the privilege of meeting and working with Dr. John Dossetor, one of Canada's prominent figures in health-care ethics. I am delighted that he has contributed the foreword for this book.

Lastly, I would like to extend a heartfelt thank you to the older adults who participated in my study. Without their willingness to share their time and their stories, this book would not exist.

encountering

DEATH AND DYING

Introduction

*One of the first steps in creating a new paradigm
for death and dying is bringing it into our lives
with greater ease and acceptance. This means
confronting death face-to-face. We cannot "fix"
death as modern medicine wants us to believe;
we can only attempt to help our loved ones
make the dying transition a more peaceful one.*

(Anderson, 2001, p. 23)

reflecting on an uneasy death

One of the transformative moments of my nursing career transpired very early in the morning as I worked the night shift on a hematology and cardiology unit. Penetrating the quiet stillness on the floor, an urgent plea for assistance was issued from the nurse responsible for patients on the west wing. I was the first to arrive to help. When I entered the room, I saw a frail, emaciated, elderly woman—breathless and pulseless—lying prostrate on the bed. In accordance with hospital policy, I began cardiopulmonary resuscitation (CPR) efforts. As I attempted to breathe life into her limp body, my lips came into contact with hers—blue, clammy, cool, and lifeless.

The code team arrived shortly thereafter and, without a moment's hesitation, sprang into action, doing precisely what they were expertly trained to do. Over the next 15 to 20 minutes, the inert woman was stabbed with large bore needles, zapped with electricity, and physically battered with chest compressions by a roomful of strangers. After an "acceptable" period of time had passed, the resuscitation efforts ceased, and the elderly woman was pronounced, simply and efficiently, dead.

My physical response was immediate and caught me off guard. I rushed to the staff bathroom where I vomited until I had nothing more to give. I was left shaking, perspiring, not quite sure what had just happened. I reached for the bottle of mouthwash, hoping to rinse the experience out of my mouth, my body, my mind. This was not the first time I had performed CPR. I was familiar with all of its various components—intubation, chest compressions, defibrillation, and so on—and I had never questioned their appropriateness. Indeed, I had witnessed a few individuals who had remarkable recoveries following CPR and continue to lead productive and satisfying lives. But this time the experience was markedly different.

It was only after the cardiac arrest concluded, and later when her family arrived at the hospital, that I learned more details of the woman's life. Her name—Edith. Her age—84. Her marital status— widow. She was a mother, a sister, a grandmother, a friend. She was terminally ill, suffering from leukemia. During the past few weeks of her hospitalization, her condition had been spiralling downwards. She and her family members were aware of her poor prognosis, and the unspoken goal of her care for the remainder of her days was to have been comfort. Unfortunately, a palliative care plan had not been initiated. A "do not resuscitate" (DNR) or "no cardiopulmonary resuscitation" (no CPR) order was never written.

My gut reaction to this situation was unwanted, unexpected, and unbelievably intense. Upon reflection, I think it represented the sense of anger, guilt, and despair I was feeling. I believed I had personally contributed to a system that failed to provide the best possible care for a patient—the level of care that every patient deserves. But perhaps the healthcare team had done even worse than that. Was it possible that we had actually breached the fundamental principle of medicine, that we had broken its golden rule: "do no harm"? Where did we go wrong? How did this happen? What could we do differently to prevent such a situation from occurring again? These questions have captured my attention and motivated my continued exploration of end-of-life decision-making for the past two decades following Edith's troubling death.

honouring martha's legacy

During my clinical experiences I also witnessed peaceful, comfortable deaths, so I knew my vision of a "good" death was not a romanticized version of reality that I had only imagined or read about. Martha had such a death. She was a 66-year-old grandmother who, like Edith, had leukemia. Her husband and two daughters, along with their husbands and young children, visited often while she was in hospital. Martha was a woman on a mission. She wanted to leave a legacy for her grandchildren and was relentless in her determination to finish recording her family history in a scrapbook, complete with pictures, letters, and other memorabilia. On videotape, she recorded messages of love and support for her family. She wanted her effervescent presence to remain alive with them after she was gone.

Martha also knew her limits. She had researched her disease thoroughly, asked many questions of her healthcare providers, and clearly articulated to her family and physician the type of care she wanted to receive under various conditions. She did not want to be resuscitated or transferred to an intensive care unit, unless the precipitating event was clearly only a temporary setback from which she was likely to recover fully. After exploring the options of receiving palliative care in her home or being transferred to a hospice setting, Martha made a conscious and informed choice to stay in the hospital where she had established quality long-term relationships with her physician, nurses on the unit, and other healthcare providers.

Alongside memories of Edith's failed resuscitation attempt, I also hold an equally vivid, but contrasting, image of Martha just a few hours before her death. She is lying comfortably in bed, propped up on either side by big fluffy pillows that her family brought from home. A bright and colourful crocheted afghan is draped over the end of her bed. There is classical music softly playing in the background. Her daughter is gently massaging her feet with lotion, its peppermint fragrance permeating the room and snuffing out the smell of hospital. Martha's husband sits quietly, reading the daily newspaper in a chair at her bedside. Her eyes are closed. Her skin is sallow and her face is gaunt, but her expression is calm with the faintest hint of a beautiful smile.

Although I met Martha before the concept of advance directives was widely known and prior to legislation supporting their use in any Canadian province, Martha had done essentially what an advance directive is intended to do. She had communicated her treatment wishes about her own end-of-life to her family and healthcare providers. She had confronted her own mortality and, taking into consideration the likely outcomes and limitations imposed on her by her unrelenting disease, had mapped out her destiny—how she wanted the rest of her life and her death to unfold. What was her experience of preparing for end-of-life? What meaning did it hold for her? How did she do it? Why did she do it? How did outlining her end-of-life treatment wishes for others help Martha to achieve the goal of dying well? I wish I had asked her these questions, but I did not. It was only in retrospect that I came to understand their significance, and I realized I had missed an incredible learning opportunity. Many individuals, even when death is imminent, do not make known their wishes regarding treatment and care at the end-of-life. Not every individual is able to confront, much less accept, his or her own mortality—healthcare providers included. Unfortunately, not everyone lives or dies well.

Although Edith's and Martha's stories represent real situations that I have encountered, names and other defining characteristics have been altered to protect the identities of the patients, their families, and my colleagues. Their stories are incomplete, in part, because of the constraints imposed by memory, language, and space, and as a protective strategy to safeguard my own psyche. Sometimes the stories are too difficult to revisit in their full measure. What makes them so hard to recount, this hesitation to fully apprehend and accept death in its entirety, is one of the threads that has become tightly woven into the text of this book.

asking the questions

My interactions with people like Edith and Martha when I was a young nurse compelled me to learn more about the experience of preparing for the end-of-life. The content of this book is largely based on the research study I undertook as part of the requirements for my doctoral degree in nursing. In that research, I sought an answer to the broad question: What is the older adult's experience of preparing an advance directive? I chose to focus on "older adults," defined as 65 years of age and older, primarily because of my clinical experiences with this age group, and because the end-of-life is expected less in younger adults. I realize now that I may have chosen this age group also because I hoped to learn something that would make a positive difference for my aging grandparents, parents, and ultimately, for myself in the distant future.

Underlying the question of how older adults prepare to write an advance directive were several other questions. What factors influence an older adult to choose to prepare an advance directive? What content do they include in their directive? Who do they consult during this process? How does this process affect their views on death and dying? How, if at all, do advance directives contribute to the objective of dying well? In the upcoming chapters of this book, the answers to these questions begin to take shape. Some questions, however, will remain unanswered because of the great mystery that is death.

In transforming my research findings from my dissertation into this book, one of my underlying goals was to make the findings of my research accessible to a wide variety of individuals. I have three particular audiences in mind: individuals (especially older adults) who are considering preparing an advance directive; family members and friends who can play a supportive role in the process; and healthcare providers who interact with older adults who have or have not prepared an advance directive.

defining the terms

Before proceeding further, it is important that I describe some of the terms that you will encounter in this book or may have encountered elsewhere—advance directives, instructional directives, proxy directives, living wills, personal directives, advance care planning. I will also provide some of the historical context for the emergence of advance directives.

Advance directives can be broadly categorized as one of two types: 1) treatment or instructional directives, or 2) proxy directives. A treatment or instructional directive is a written document that individuals execute while capable in which they state their wishes regarding healthcare should they become unable to make decisions for themselves (Backlar & McFarland, 1996; Browne & Sullivan, 2006; Degrazia, 1999; de Raeve, 1993; Kelley, 1995; Leslie & Badzek, 1996; Perrin, 1997; Yamani, Fleming, Brensilver, & Brandstetter, 1995). In a proxy directive, capable individuals appoint a person or persons to make healthcare decisions for them should they become unable to do so (Browne & Sullivan, 2006; de Raeve, 1993; Kelley, 1995; Perrin, 1997). Depending on the jurisdiction, the appointed individual(s) may be referred to by terms such as a healthcare proxy, attorney for healthcare, substitute decision-maker, or agent.

You may also have come across the term "living will." This phrase is sometimes used interchangeably with "advance directive," particularly in the United States. Historically, in Canada, living wills were usually limited to addressing the issue of treatment refusals in the context of terminal illness or imminent death. A living will typically remains a standardized document that includes general statements instructing that an individual not be kept alive by artificial means or heroic measures. For example, in a living will, you might find a statement such as, "I do not wish to be hooked up to a machine that would breathe for me (mechanical ventilator) should I have a terminal illness such as cancer." In contrast to most living wills, a treatment or instructional advance directive allows individuals to indicate various types of medical treatment that they do or do not want. They may also address situations of chronic illness or injuries that do not reflect what we would usually define as life-threatening or terminal. Living wills and advance directives are most often conceptualized as written documents.

There is a wide variation in the legislation concerning advance directives and living wills, particularly in the areas of age requirements for both makers of directives and proxies, dating and witnessing requirements, involvement of lawyers, and restrictions regarding the type of treatment decisions that can be made by a proxy (Browne & Sullivan, 2006). In Alberta, where the study I conducted was based, advance directives include both treatment and proxy directives and are referred to as personal directives. Alberta's *Personal Directives Act* (1996) does not grant authority to proxies to make decisions related to certain medical treatments such as psychosurgery, sterilization that is not medically necessary, removal of tissue from the maker's living body, or participation in research that offers little or no potential benefit to the individual, unless the personal directive contains clear instructions about these matters. Both the maker of the directive and the person appointed as proxy must be 18 years of age or older. To be legally recognized in Alberta, the document must be completed in writing, signed, dated, and witnessed.

One commonality across all jurisdictions is that advance directives come into effect only when their maker becomes incapacitated and is no longer capable of making decisions on his or her own behalf.

As long as an individual is able to make decisions about his or her treatment, informed consent is sought from the individual and what is written in an advance directive is immaterial.

The term "advance care planning" focusses on an ongoing process of planning for the end-of-life that emphasizes communication between individuals, their substitute decision-makers, and their healthcare providers, and encompasses the preparation of advance directives (personal directives) and living wills as part of the process (Karel, Moye, Bank, & Azar, 2007; Murray, Sheikh, & Thomas, 2006). While advance directives generally focus on medical treatment decisions, advance care planning may also take into consideration other personal choices such as where an individual wishes to live and how one's money should be managed.

For reasons that are not entirely clear, the term "living will" has fallen somewhat out of favour. The terms "advance directive" and "advance care planning" are more often used now in the literature and in practice. Throughout the book, I use the terms "advance directive" and "personal directive" interchangeably. In the last chapter of this book, I'll explain why I chose to use the less popular term "living will" in the title of my book.

tracing the history

The concept of advance directives has been around since the mid-1970s. At that time, life-sustaining technologies had progressed to the point where individuals with life-threatening conditions, previously untreatable and fatal, could now be kept alive for indefinite periods of time. The factors that stimulated the development of advance directives include the development of new life-sustaining technologies, rising healthcare costs, an aging population, raised consumer awareness about health matters, and increased healthcare litigation (de Raeve, 1993; Johns, 1996; Kelley, 1995; Matzo, 1997; Ross & West, 1995). This set of conditions is most evident in a Western, and particularly a North American, context and thus advance directives are primarily a Western phenomenon.

As you read this book, it is important to be mindful that our ability to engage in a discussion about treatment wishes and preferences at the end-of-life is a matter of great privilege as many individuals in the world struggle for daily survival and have limited or no access to even the most primitive kinds of life-sustaining treatments (such as clean water and nutritious food). The vast majority of philosophical and empirical publications about advance directives (and there are literally thousands) originate in North America. The approach to advance directives in North America has been predominantly legal-istic and largely premised on the notion of personal autonomy—the right to make choices about what happens to one's body and self. Autonomy is a principle that is highly valued and fiercely protected in the Western world.

In North America, the number of individuals reported to have completed an advance directive ranges from 2 to 41 percent, depending on the group studied (Dooley & Marsden, 1994; Eman-uel & Emanuel, 1989; Heffner, Fahy, & Barbieri, 1996; Hamel, Guse, Hawranik, & Bond, 2002; High, 1993a; High, 1993b; Ho, Thiel, Rubin, & Singer, 2000; Johns, 1996; Leslie & Badzek, 1996; Ott, 1999; Perrin, 1997; Ross & West, 1995; Thorevska, Tilluckdharry, Tickoo, Havasi, Amoateng-Adjepong, & Manthous, 2005). This statistic stands in juxtaposition to the findings that between 60 and 90 percent of the population consider making their wishes known through an advance directive to be a useful and relevant exercise and that most would be interested in completing such a document (Anderson, Walker, Pierce, & Mills, 1986; Johns, 1996; Mendelssohn & Singer, 1994; Molloy, Guyatt, Alemayehu, & McIlroy, 1991; Nicolasora et al., 2006; Sam & Singer, 1993). Although a number of philosophical, per-sonal, and practical barriers to completing an advance directive have been discussed in the literature, they do not seem to account fully for this large discrepancy between attitudes and behaviours.

exploring the benefits and barriers

The primary purpose of an advance directive is to allow individuals during conditions of incapacity to maintain control over decisions affecting their treatment and care (Collins, Parks, & Winter, 2006). A secondary purpose, as described in the literature, is to reduce feelings of burden and guilt for family members and healthcare providers (Backlar & McFarland, 1996; Colvin, Myhre, Welch, & Hammes, 1993; Downie, 1992; Kuhse, 1999; Mendelssohn & Singer, 1994; Sawchuck & Ross Kerr, 2000). The feeling of burden for the maker of the directive may also be reduced.

Individuals who have completed an advance directive often report that it gives them peace of mind to know that they have done what they can to ensure that their end-of-life will proceed as they have directed (Colvin et al., 1993; Dooley & Marsden, 1994; Leslie & Badzek, 1996; Mendelssohn & Singer, 1994). Some individuals may also feel better informed and prepared to face their death as a result of discussing death and dying while completing their own advance directive (Downie, 1992). Another potential benefit is when individuals engage in a dialogue about their advance directives with their family members, friends, and healthcare providers, these relationships may be strengthened and improved (Backlar & McFarland, 1996; Johns, 1996).

Much has been written on the philosophical, personal, and practical barriers to completing advance directives. Here, I am going to touch briefly on the main concerns. One of the most persistent arguments against using advance directives is a philosophical one, centred on the notion of personhood and the concern that who we are as a person may change over time (Degrazia, 1999; de Raeve, 1993; Downie, 1992; Kuhse, 1999; May, 1997; Mendelssohn & Singer, 1994; Tonelli, 1996). The fear is that what an individual records in her advance directive at one point in time, when she is healthy and capable, may not accurately reflect her wishes at a later point when she is ill and incapable. A related issue is that of uncertainty, the idea that it is impossible for an individual to predict or imagine the future and one's response to unforeseen situations (Colvin et al., 1991; de Raeve, 1993; Kuhse, 1999; Sam & Singer, 1993; Tonelli, 1996; Winland-Brown, 1998).

It is known that some individuals change their minds when actually confronted with a particular situation (Downie, 1992; Shore, Rubin, Haisfield, McGuire, Zabora, & Krumm, 1993). For example, a young man who previously stated that under no circumstances would he want to be hooked up to machines experiences quadriplegia following a diving accident. He now requires mechanical ventilation to remain alive, and says, "I want to live; don't disconnect me from this machine." Such an example, although relevant, is somewhat moot because the individual's advance directive ought not to be considered as long as the individual is still capable of consenting to treatment and making his own decisions. We do have a right to change our minds. Throughout life, who we are as a person is continually being shaped by our experiences, but I would argue that there is some continuity of personhood that remains over time. We may describe an elderly woman with advanced dementia as a "different" person than the one we knew before her illness, but she remains able to recall events from her past that continue to inform who she is today.

These concerns about personhood, uncertainty, and changing one's mind are valid and need to be considered as limitations when one is preparing an advance directive. However, given that we have limited alternative ways of knowing an individual's current wishes once he or she becomes incapacitated, previously expressed capable wishes may be the closest facsimile available to us. In other words, when an individual is unable to communicate his or her treatment preferences to us, an advance directive containing instructions that can be interpreted by a trusted proxy who knew the individual well may be the best guide available.

There are also pragmatic issues. A lack of clarity, insufficient specificity, and ambiguity in the wording of life-sustaining treatment preferences are frequently cited as problems associated with instructional or treatment directives (Dooley & Marsden, 1994; Downie, 1992; Institute of Medical Ethics, 1993; Johns, 1996; Kuhse, 1999; Perrin, 1997; Ross & West, 1995; Teno, Licks et al., 1997). Proxy directives have limitations as well. Not everyone has a suitable substitute decision-maker within his or her network of family and friends (Backlar & McFarland, 1996; Sam & Singer, 1993). Additionally, if there were no meaningful and comprehensive discussions between the makers of directives and their surrogates, it is unlikely that they will be able to represent the patient's healthcare preferences accurately. There is some evidence of discordance between individuals' and proxies' understanding of treatment preferences noted in the literature (Doukas & McCullough, 2001; Hardingham, 1997; Hayley, Cassel, Snyder, & Rudberg, 1996; Kelley, 1995; Levenson & Pettrey, 1994; Perrin, 1997; Sansone & Phillips, 1995; Yamani et al., 1995).

Other factors identified as barriers to completing advance directives are a lack of knowledge, beliefs about death and dying (personal, cultural, religious), fear of death, fear of abandonment, limited access to the document, reluctance of healthcare providers to engage in conversations about advance directives, lack of time for conversations, and procrastination (Ackerman, 1997; Berrio & Levesque, 1996; Hoffman, Zimmerman, & Tompkins, 1997; Johns, 1996; Pearlman, 1996; Perrin, 1997; Winland-Brown, 1998; Wood & DelPapa, 1996).

Unlike the philosophical concerns that were raised, there are identifiable and practical solutions for most of the pragmatic barriers identified here, such as providing adequate information and education to the public, training healthcare providers in how to engage in end-of-life conversations, and putting in place processes to ensure documentation is readily accessible when needed.

setting the stage

Despite the philosophical, practical, and personal barriers described in the previous section, there remain a number of reasons that preparing an advance directive might be considered a valuable enterprise, particularly for the older adult. First, most people who die are over the age of 65. Most desire a good death, one that is as pain free and comfortable as possible, and one in which they are able to maintain some control. Second, as many as 70 percent of all individuals may be faced with a decision to withhold life-sustaining treatment at some point in their life (Kelley, 1995; Matzo, 1997). Third, the average 65 year old in Canada has a life expectancy of an additional 18 years, the last few of which are often accompanied by chronic illnesses and varying levels of disability (Fisher, Ross, & Maclean, 2000). As a result of illness and/or cognitive impairment, a significant number of individuals will not be able to be involved fully in decision-making at the end-of-life. Unless individuals share their wishes with others in advance, it is not possible to ensure that they will be carried out.

introducing alice

In Chapter 1, you will meet Alice Dawson. Alice is a fictitious character that represents an amalgam of the 15 older adults that I interviewed in my study. Most of what Alice says comes from transcripts of the conversations I had with individuals who had completed their own advance directives. (The guiding questions for our conversations are included in Appendix A.) Through Alice's voice and the accompanying text, I describe five general themes that emerged: protecting self and others, facing one's mortality, talking about death, choosing an ally, and getting it done.

My goal in writing Alice's story is to blend the voices of many into one coherent and articulate voice that shows the experience of preparing an advance directive. I hope that Alice's story will draw you closer to this experience. If you are an individual, particularly an older adult, who has already completed your own advance directive, what I have written may resonate with what you have already experienced and stimulate new areas for consideration. If you have not yet contemplated your own wishes for the end-of-life, you may gain insight into the process and be stimulated to engage in a dialogue about advance care planning with yourself and others. Similarly, healthcare providers, family members, and friends may acquire a greater understanding of the experience of advance care planning and be in a better position to support and collaborate with individuals who are contemplating such decisions.

A special *typeface* will signify when Alice is speaking. After each segment of Alice's narrative, I respond by questioning, interpreting, and discussing what she has just said. At times, these reflections take me to other data sources both in and beyond my study. These sources include quotations from the transcripts of study participants, references to the scientific literature, and explorations of fictional accounts that illuminate some aspect of preparing an advance directive. You may want to begin by reading Alice's story in its entirety first, omitting what I have written in between. But I trust you will eventually return to read the intervening sections so that together we can strive to discover and understand the experience of completing an advance directive.

While living through the various phases of this study from conception to completion, my own attempts to understand death in a meaningful way occurred alongside those of the participants. In this book, I endeavour to remain true to the spirit of their individual stories. If through reading this account, you gain a greater awareness, appreciation, and understanding of the older adult's experience of preparing an advance directive, I will have achieved my primary goal. If it inspires an ethical response (helps you to do the right thing) in your next encounter with an older adult who has or is engaged in the process of end-of-life decision-making, it will have been doubly successful. Lastly, if the writing evokes a sense of wonder about preparing for your own end-of-life, if it causes you to silently ponder the way you live out each day, and if it stimulates new questions for you about life and death—thoughtful questions that you have never considered before—then my ultimate aspirations for writing this book will have been realized.

protecting

SELF AND OTHERS

1

*Maman had an old relative who had been
kept alive in a coma for the last six months.
"I hope you wouldn't let them keep me going
like that," she had said to us. "It's horrible!"
If Dr. N. took it into his head to beat a record
he would be a dangerous opponent.*

(de Beauvoir, 1965, p. 53)

noticing advance directives

Every year around this time, I spend an evening sorting through my personal documents, looking to see if there is anything I need to change or update. And tonight's the lucky night! As I leaf through one of several file folders tucked away in a fireproof security box, an old church bulletin falls to the floor. The notice printed boldly on the back page jumps out at me:

> *"Choosing Now for the Future"*
> *Information Session on Advance Directives*
> *Speaker: Jack Brown (Lawyer)*
> *Tuesday, February 26 at 7:00 p.m.*
> *Everyone welcome.*

Believe it or not, it was at this information session that I made the decision to complete my own advance directive. I'm not sure why I've held on to this church bulletin for so long, but it brings back a flood of memories. When I first saw this notice, I didn't know much about advance directives, but I had heard a report on the radio that there was a new law here in Alberta that had something to do with them. From what I gathered, advance directives had to do with me having a say in the kind of care and treatment I wanted to receive. That sounded like a good thing. At least it was enough of an enticement at the time to secure my attendance at that information session (and for me to forgo my line-dancing class that week).

Perhaps before I go any further, I should introduce myself. My name is Alice Dawson. I am 74 years old—although most say I don't look a day over 69! My husband of more than 40 years, Stuart, died just over three years ago. (Has it really been that long? There are still days when a waft of his cologne catches me by surprise. When I turn to look at him, he isn't there.) His death was long and drawn out—cancer—multiple myeloma they called it. If you must know, the whole situation was horrible, but I'm not ready to tell you about that just yet.

Together, we had three children—two girls and a boy. Funny, how I still think of them that way, as my girls and boy, but they are grown up with children of their own—my grandchildren, six in total. Now my grandchildren are entering adulthood. It's hard to believe so much time has passed. So many things have changed. But some things have stayed the same. Take my home for instance. Can you believe that I still live in the same house that Stuart and I raised our family in, here in the city? It's starting to be a bit much for me to look after with the cleaning and yard work, but it's so nice to have the extra space when my family comes to visit, and there's something to be said about being in familiar surroundings. It makes me feel good, secure. I have a lot of friends who live close by, too. Almost everything I need is within walking distance—the grocery store, restaurants, the church, the community centre. If I need to drive somewhere, I can. My car has a few kilometres under its belt, but it's in good shape and dependable, and I'm proud to say my driving record is accident free. I'm not ready to move just yet. For now, I'm happy right where I am.

Let me think. What else is important for you to know about me? I suppose I should tell you that I was an elementary school teacher. I worked in a rural school teaching Grades 1 to 8, until my oldest daughter, Susan, was born. Then we moved into the city, and I became a stay-at-home mom. A few years later David arrived, and then the youngest, my baby, Christine. It was only when Christine started high school that I re-entered the work world and spent another 20 years or so standing at the front of a classroom. I've been retired now for about 10 years, but it seems like I'm busier than ever. Mondays—volunteering with the hospital auxiliary; Tuesdays—line-dancing class; Wednesdays—lunch with several of my long-time friends; Thursdays—choir practice; and on it goes. Then there are all of my family activities—watching my grandsons and granddaughters play hockey (I told you times had changed), birthday parties, school concerts, graduations, and the like.

Unlike going to school, getting married, or having a child, preparing an advance directive is not an experience that most people are likely to encounter as they go about their routine activities of daily living. Gaining awareness about advance directives requires a different kind of exposure. The ways in which older adults come to be aware of advance directives and factors that influence their completion is perhaps best captured under the theme of protecting self and others.

The older adults who participated in the study I conducted learned about advance directives in a variety of ways. For many, like Alice, their knowledge about the existence of advance directives was first raised through media exposure. One of the study participants described how she followed the Karen Ann Quinlan case in the United States for a number of years, and it was through such news coverage that she learned about living wills and later advance directives. Quinlan was a young woman who, following a drug overdose, was in a persistent vegetative state requiring respirator support. Strongly believing that their daughter would not have wished to continue living in this condition, her parents successfully petitioned the courts for her father to become her guardian and decision-maker so that he could make a decision to withdraw the respirator. One participant's response to the publicity was quite clear: "I certainly don't want to be hooked up to a machine. [After] hearing stories on TV about people in that situation and what a difficult position it was for doctors, and for family too, when they didn't know what you wanted done. So I decided that I didn't want to be in that situation." For this participant, the media was not only a source of information about advance directives, but a trigger for her desire to complete her own directive.

More recently, the case of Terri Schiavo brought once again to the public's attention the issue of withdrawal of life-sustaining treatment (Kollas & Boyer-Kollas, 2006). Schiavo was a young woman who suffered a severe brain injury following cardiac arrest. She was fully dependent on others for her care and was fed through a feeding tube. Her husband believed that withdrawal of the feeding tube was what Shiavo would have wanted; her parents vehemently disagreed. Shiavo had not completed a written living will (advance directive). Unfortunately her tragic case became a media spectacle, with politicians, religious leaders, lobby groups, and the public all becoming involved and weighing in with their opinions. One of the responses to this case has been a marked increase in the number of requests for information about living wills and assistance in preparing living wills by lawyers and medical practitioners in the United States (Crable, 2005).

On occasion, it was family members who introduced the study participants to the notion of advance directives. It is likely that family members found out about advance directives through the media as well, but this was not directly explored in my study. Others found out about advance directives from their lawyers during an appointment for other business, most often completion of an estate will. Questions have been raised about the appropriateness of the involvement of lawyers and the legal profession in the process of advance directive preparation (Singer, 1995). There are concerns that the spirit of an advance directive will become entangled in legalistic and technical language and bureaucracy (Gamble, McDonald, & Lichstein, 1991). Others are worried that lawyers may not be able to inform their clients adequately about the healthcare decisions they wish to include in their written directives (Singer, 1995). Do lawyers have the necessary expertise to lead a discussion about death and dying? Will the resulting document be meaningful, relevant, or useful in a healthcare context? Why has this document about life and death, natural occurrences, become infused with legalese?

Several participants in the study I conducted had prepared their directives in consultation with a lawyer, but not just any lawyer. It seemed important for them to have had a sustained and positive relationship with their lawyer (or to have been referred to the lawyer by someone they trusted who indicated that he or she had a good reputation) prior to including the lawyer in the process. For some, hiring a lawyer was the last step in the process. After preparing their directives, these participants wanted someone to confirm that their document was written in accordance with the law. They wanted someone to give their document an official stamp of approval. They did not want a technicality to interfere with the enactment of their directive. One participant outlined a history of broken promises within her family. She believed that it was important to have her decisions written down and legally approved so that history would not repeat itself. She said, "There were a lot of problems with myself growing up. I came from a broken family and then came from a blended family, which didn't blend too well. It was like oil and water...Nothing [major decisions such as division of the estate] was done on paper...If it's not on paper, I mean, you may be brothers and sisters but you don't always think alike."

For some, the exposure to information about advance directives came about serendipitously. One participant regularly attended support group meetings for family members of residents in the nursing home where his elderly 97-year-old mother resided. At each meeting, there was an educational component. His introduction to advance directives came about this way. "I think we were kind of running thin on subject material but one day one of the nurses mentioned personal directives and asked us if we would be interested. We didn't want to say no because we didn't know anything about it and didn't want to make her feel bad so we said yes and that triggered the first meeting...and what a wonderful meeting it was." This was one of two participants who identified a health professional, a nurse, as the person who first introduced the notion of advance directives to them. The other participant was part of a walking group that also included a nurse. As this participant said, "I have a walking group on Wednesdays and one of the gals is a nurse. She brought it up a couple of times that they were, you know, expected to ask this [if patients have an advance directive] all the time of people. And she was kind of gently nudging us that maybe we should be doing this. And again, as I said, because I'm a widow, you know, there isn't somebody right here who would make these decisions so it seemed a good idea."

A few were not sure where or when they had first become aware of advance directives. One participant who lived in a senior's apartment building stated, "I don't really know first off where I heard about it. I know we had some meetings downstairs. You know, people have come and spoken on it."

I pause to consider my own introduction to advance directives. They have been a part of my consciousness now for so many years that I cannot recall an exact moment, yet I suspect it was during my undergraduate nursing education in the early 1980s. I can imagine it happening in the context of a clinical discussion about continuing life-sustaining treatment for a seriously ill individual whose prognosis is grim. I can visualize a group of nursing students around a conference table nodding their heads in agreement—if the individual indicated no heroic measures in his or her living will, the treatment should be stopped; the individual should be allowed to die. At that time, however, neither living wills nor advance directives were legally sanctioned documents in the province where I was studying. A more personal introduction came later, after I had been in nursing practice for several years.

After being prompted by the media, a lawyer, a family member, or another person, several study participants sought further information by attending presentations or workshops in locations like Senior's Centres or church basements. Participants frequently identified the church as a location for information sessions. Churches have been identified as a common gathering place for healthcare consumers (Sanderson, 1995). The role of the church may be more significant than the paucity of literature in this area would suggest. Indeed the involvement of religious organizations or leaders in the process of preparing directives is rarely mentioned. One wonders if those who attend such seminars interpret the church's provision of a venue for information sessions and discussions as an endorsement of advance directives. Are those who participate in information sessions held in religious facilities more likely to complete a directive than those who receive information in a different, less orthodox, venue? If individuals do not have a religious affiliation, is their access to information about advance directives more limited? These are questions for further consideration. Religious leaders are, on some occasions, suggested as a person to talk to about completing an advance directive, particularly in the absence of family members (Heydemann, 1997). The extent of knowledge that religious leaders have about advance directives has not been reported in the literature, but one might speculate that their educational background would prepare them well to engage in discussions about the concept of mortality and facing one's own death. Their expertise in helping individuals make specific treatment decisions is, however, likely to be more limited.

What was surprising to me in the participants' stories was the relative invisibility of healthcare providers in the process of raising awareness or providing information about advance directives. A few individuals reported talking informally to family members or friends who were in health professions, nurses in particular. One participant was considering seeking specific information from her family doctor, but had not yet done so. Before making a decision about whether or not she wanted to be resuscitated, she wanted a medical opinion regarding her chances of surviving cardiopulmonary resuscitation, given her current health status. Another had asked her physician about her cancer prognosis. After formulating their directives, several participants provided their physicians with a copy and briefly discussed its contents with them. Given that healthcare professionals are a group who could provide relevant information to individuals who are making decisions about their future healthcare, why is it that they are not initiating discussions about advance directives? A partial answer to that question is foreshadowed in the quotation that opens this chapter: "Dr. N...would be a dangerous opponent," and will become clearer as Alice continues her story.

focussing on the future

Rewind now to Tuesday, 6:45 p.m. The church basement is starting to fill; there must be at least 30 to 40 members of the congregation here. People of all ages are in attendance, but most are sporting white or grey hair. My daughter Susan has accompanied me, for moral support I suppose. Not that I am concerned that I'll need it, but you never know. I've been known in the past to get a bit emotional, so it's nice to have someone familiar around. Let's face it, I am getting older (you don't know how hard that is for me to admit; to see it permanently inked on this paper is even more inconceivable).

Tonight the discussion is going to focus on the future, and for me, death is a real part of that future. I don't like to think about my own death. Actually, let me take that back. It's not my death that worries me. It's dying. I think death is just the beginning of another great adventure, a time where I will be reunited with my beloved Stuart, my parents, his parents, and others who have passed before, maybe even the puppy I had when I was a kid, Speckles! Who knows? But dying? If I had a choice, I'd skip that part of the process. You see, as I told you earlier, I watched my husband die, little by little, and I wish that experience on no one. I don't know if it was harder on him or me and the rest of the family. We all felt so helpless.

An advance directive is a future-oriented concept. It requires individuals to extrapolate their current thoughts and beliefs into some imagined future time and place. I wonder if an individual whose approach to life is to attend fully to the present—the here and the now—would be able to prepare an advance directive. Or would that person say, as so many people do, that he will complete a directive when he is sicker or older (High, 1993b; Perrin, 1997; Winland-Brown, 1998)? When I met with two of the study participants, they were struggling with making the final edits to their advance directives. One participant said, "I'm not sure what the procrastination is all about—I think my good health. If I were still sick, it would be finished." Many months have passed and I am still waiting to receive a copy of their finished products.

Alice describes death as a great adventure. I wonder how one's conceptualization of death affects one's ability to complete a directive. If one does not picture death as a great adventure, is it more difficult to complete an advance directive? Is it important—necessary—to have supportive family members or friends with whom a vision of the future can be shared? These are questions that will resurface again later as Alice's story is revealed in greater detail.

listening attentively

Conversation is buzzing throughout the room, the usual chit-chat about the cold weather and the snow that has fallen in the past 24 hours. One of this evening's organizers raps loudly on the table to get our attention. The presenter, Jack Brown, is introduced. He proceeds to tell us what he knows about advance directives and of his experience in assisting individuals in their preparation. I listen closely, attentively. He tells us:

> *An advance directive, or personal directive (as it is referred to in Alberta's legislation) allows individuals to do one or both of the following:*
> 1) *you can provide written instructions about the type of care you want to receive should you become incapacitated and unable to make decisions for yourself; for instance, you might indicate whether or not you would want to be maintained on a respirator if you were terminally ill, and/or*
> 2) *you can name an individual(s) to be responsible for making decisions on your behalf should you become incapable of doing so; this person is referred to as an agent.*

So far, so good. Out of the corner of my eye, I notice a man in the row ahead shifting uncomfortably in his seat. I turn my head to get a better look at his face. It's Jim, a long-time member of the congregation. A single tear is rolling down his cheek. His wife, Rose, died not long ago—I suppose it's been a month or two. She'd suffered from Alzheimer's disease for years and at the end wasn't able to do anything for herself. Jim was so faithful to her, so good to her. He cared for her at home until almost the end. He fed her, bathed her, even changed her incontinence briefs—things I don't imagine he did for his own children. I wonder what he's thinking right now, what he thinks about this whole advance directive idea. I wonder if Rose had an advance directive. I wonder if they had ever talked about the possibility of one of them becoming sick. I wonder if he had ever imagined he would be the one doing the caregiving, that he would outlive Rose. So many unanswered questions. I need to talk about these things with my family...

A poke in the ribs from my daughter brings me back to the room. I guess she'd noticed my attention drifting. I am back now, listening to the words of the speaker. Mr. Brown goes on to say that an individual can include instructions not only about healthcare issues, but also about accommodation, who the person may live and associate with, participation in social, educational, and employment activities, and legal matters— every kind of personal matter except those that have to do with money. You need another type of document to deal with financial matters: a power of attorney for property.

No matter how interested we are in the information being shared by a speaker, it is the human or relational side of a story that seems most likely to capture our attention. Alice is listening carefully to the lawyer, trying to take in what he has to say about advance directives, yet a subtle movement and single tear has taken her to an entirely different place—one where relationships are of utmost importance. From imagining the relationship between Jim and Rose, she moves to contemplating her own relationships with her family and expresses her motivation to act—to talk to them. This notion of talking about death will be expanded upon later.

In describing one aspect of the Alberta legislation, the lawyer talks about the notion of an agent. I wonder why the word "agent" was chosen to signify the person who would represent the wishes of the incapacitated individual. For me, the word conjures images of

James Bond, Agent 007. He always had some gadget or gizmo that he pulled out in time to save the day. Is this the kind of agent one would want making decisions about what happens to them? I shudder at the thought. How does the way we label things influence the way we think and act? What if this substitute decision-maker had been named a partner, a collaborator, or an ally instead of an agent in the legislation? Would that make any difference?

The word "agent" has a legalistic or business connotation. Indeed an agent is defined as a person who provides a specific service, or a person who acts for another in business, politics, and so forth (Barber, 2001). For me, the term also holds a notion of concealment as in undercover agent or secret agent. What is absent from the definition is any ethical or relational component. There is the sense that the person named has the right to speak and act on the individual's behalf. The notion, however, that the agent is connected to the individual in a more meaningful way is not evident. The moral obligation of the agent to carry out the individual's wishes seems less explicit. Alternatively, words like ally or partner emphasize an association or connection, a relationship, between two or more individuals working together toward some common end. An ally is defined as a person or organization that co-operates with or helps another. Similarly, a partner is defined as a person who shares or takes part with another or others in some activity (Barber, 2001). This experience of choosing an agent, the individual responsible for making decisions for the older adult should he or she become incapacitated, will be explored more fully as Alice's story continues.

desiring comfort and peace

After outlining for us what an advance directive is, the lawyer goes on to tell us some reasons for completing a directive that we might want to consider. First, he says, it is a way of guaranteeing, at least to a certain extent, that life after we become incapacitated, including our dying, unfolds in the way we want it to. My desire is that it will be as comfortable and peaceful as possible—if that means giving me pain medication to knock me out, do it; if it means that I'll die a bit sooner, that's okay; I do not want to linger. I want to leave this world with my strong sense of pride and dignity intact. And, by the way, I want to know what's going on—if I've got cancer and only a few months to live, you better tell me. I want to know. I need to know. Second, he suggests that preparing a directive might reduce the burden on family members and the healthcare system so that difficult decisions don't have to be made by family members or doctors and nurses in times of crisis at the bedside.

To illustrate his points, the lawyer tells us about a situation he encountered in which an advance directive had not been prepared. Mr. S., as he called him, had a terminal illness. It was anticipated that he would die within the next few months. During his hospitalization, he developed life-threatening pneumonia. The healthcare team indicated to the family that one available option was not to treat the pneumonia. His son, who lived close by and had been with his father throughout many of his earlier cancer treatments, agreed with this course of action. He believed his father would not want to undergo further invasive treatments. The man's daughter, who had flown in from abroad, thought that everything should be done to save her father, including admission to an intensive care unit and ventilator support. (Save him from what? I silently wondered.)

Unfortunately, Mr. S. was so sick that he was unable to be involved in the decision-making process. No discussions about this sort of scenario had taken place, although his son recalled that Mr. S. had told him early on in the course of his illness that he didn't want any "heroics." The healthcare providers were unsure how to proceed. If Mr. S. had documented his wishes in a directive or named someone to be his decision-maker, a more expedient and timely resolution to this dilemma might have been achieved.

The lawyer's arguments are persuasive, and my resolve to take on the task of completing my own advance directive is cemented that evening. Susan agrees that this is a worthwhile pursuit.

Protecting themselves from physical pain was one of the underlying motivations that many study participants verbalized as a reason for completing a directive. The goal of having a pain free dying process seems fairly straightforward. Our bodies and minds have been designed and conditioned to avoid pain. When we accidentally touch the hot burner on the stove, our hand withdraws automatically before we can even mentally register what has happened. It seems understandable that we would want to continue this pattern of avoiding pain while we approach death. There are those who have a redemptive view of pain, an extrapolation of the "no pain, no gain" adage, but most participants in my study were not strong proponents of that belief. Some participants were even willing to trade days of life for assurances of pain relief. Quoting directly from his directive, one participant stated, "I wish to be kept comfortable and free from pain and this means that I may be given pain medication even though it may dull consciousness and directly shorten my life." Similar phrasing appeared in several participants' directives. Another said, "But I certainly don't like pain, so if I couldn't manage the pain myself I would want painkillers, without some staff member worrying about whether I was going to get addicted because that is ludicrous to worry about addiction when somebody is dying."

Participants shared distressing and heartbreaking stories about family and friends who had suffered tremendous pain at the end-of-life. One participant stated, "I really feel that people should be allowed to die when they are in agony. I cannot bear the thought of that happening to me, and I can't bear the thought of any other loved one going through what my friend did just in February. I just think that is absolutely barbaric!" Another recounted, "He was right there, right in front of the nurses' station. And when I went in there he was throwing up and he was having a bowel movement and he was in tremendous pain and he said, 'Hi, I'm sorry...I'm sorry.' And I knew he wanted me to leave. And I went out and asked for help and just then his wife came along the corridor and a nurse came, but he was in agony. And he was a man with a tremendously high pain tolerance."

Given the discouraging accounts about inadequate control of pain at the end-of-life that are reported in the literature (for example, Freeborne, Lynn, & Desbiens, 2000; Lo, 1995) and that were sadly reaffirmed in the stories of participants, two questions come immediately to mind. First, why do health professionals manage controlling pain at the end-of-life so poorly? Second, will stating in writing one's wishes for pain control have any impact on practice? An additional question of an entirely different nature is also triggered. Just as pain is a part of natural childbirth, is it possible that pain is a part of the natural dying process? In childbirth, the pain results in the birth of a child, which is typically a joyful occasion. In death, might there be some similarly positive outcome to pain— one that would make enduring or witnessing the pain more tolerable, even a worthwhile endeavour? Florence Scott-Maxwell

(1968), reflecting on her life, suggests a further linkage between death and birth. She says, "I remember that in the last months of my pregnancies the child seemed to claim almost all my body, my strength, my breath, and I held on wondering if my burden was my enemy, uncertain as to whether my life was at all mine. Is life a pregnancy? That would make death a birth" (p. 76). Another author in describing the experience of her mother's death also uses the analogy of birth. She says her mother's death "was like birth—the fear, the pain, the loss of control, the immense vulnerability, Mom's awareness that she was moving into the realm of spirit, the rhythmic breathing, the deliverance. We sisters were midwives. We knew that as her breath deepened, grew rhythmic, Mom gave birth to her own beautiful soul" (Shaw-MacKinnon, 2001, p. 228). There is something comforting to me about the birth metaphor—I find the images quite moving, even beautiful. I wonder if sharing this description of death would be helpful to those who are suffering at the end-of-life.

The notion of dignity was one that surfaced again and again in the conversations I had with study participants. When asked to describe what they meant when they used this term, they talked about concepts such as being independent, being respected, being listened to, and being heard. For instance, one participant said, "My husband lost his dignity, his independence and his pride, because he was totally dependent on them [the healthcare team] and they made the decisions." Participants told disturbing stories of older people who had been treated poorly and disrespectfully, in part, because of their age and inability to speak or defend themselves. One participant recalled seeing a man publicly chastise his frail and elderly wife who was in a wheelchair for asking for assistance to be taken to the bathroom during a hair appointment. The participant said, "You see treatment like this of old people, it's disgraceful." They talked about a society where elderly persons are devalued and their life experiences and accumulated wisdom dismissed because of agist attitudes. What they spoke of is well recorded in the literature (for example, Kilner, 1990; Fisher et al., 2000), but to hear its confirmation in their personal stories was disheartening. It raises many more questions outside the scope of this book. How can a transformation in society's negative aging stereotypes be accomplished? What roles have family members and healthcare providers played in perpetuating these negative stereotypes? What roles can they play in eliminating them?

experiencing the death and dying of a loved one

Remember when I said earlier that it was the dying process, not death, that frightens me the most? I think now is the time to tell you where my fears about dying stem from. The first person I ever saw die was my mother. I was 10 or 11 at the time. I never found out what was wrong with her—it just seemed like her parts wore out. I remember her face contorted in pain, her body curled up in a fetal position on the bed that had been moved into the front room on the main floor of our house. Her perpetual moaning was often the last sound I heard while I drifted off to sleep. When my mother died, we were all there—my dad, my grandmother, the doctor, my brothers, my sister. Her body relaxed, and the look of anguish on her face miraculously vanished. Finally there was a sense of peace, a sigh of relief. Although I knew my mother was dead and I should be sad, what I felt inside was a sort of happiness. Without understanding how or why, I intuitively felt that she was now in a better place.

The only other person I have watched die is my husband, Stuart. After being diagnosed with multiple myeloma, my stalwart husband, my Rock of Gibraltar, slowly crumbled before my eyes. It began as a rather benign (did that ever turn out to be the wrong word) pain in his hip. Before we knew it, he was receiving chemotherapy and his body was fighting for its life. I didn't know a person could throw up so much, that diarrhea could last forever, that the skin's surface could break down so quickly and expansively. The chemotherapy gave him a short reprieve from the aggressive disease, but it was not long before his cancer returned. As if he hadn't suffered enough, the next phase of the disease caused intractable pain. Near the end, even with the gentlest of hands, it was impossible to turn him or even touch him without hurting him. No amount of pain medication worked. The doctors seemed eager to keep trying new combinations of drugs to try to stop the disease. Nobody talked about his death. Not the doctors. Not the nurses. Not my husband. Not me. Then one day as I sat knitting at his bedside, he made a horrible gasping sound and suddenly stopped breathing.

I was alone in the hospital room with him. I didn't know what to do. I pressed the call bell and yelled for someone to come, to help. They came. En masse. They put a tube down his throat. They pumped on his chest. They *attached wires to his body. They poked him with needles. I was standing huddled in the corner, my back against the wall, feeling small, forgotten. I was unable to speak, but inside I was screaming—"Stop! Don't hurt him anymore!" Tears were streaming down my cheeks; I couldn't breathe. Finally someone said, "It's time to call it." As quickly as the commotion had begun, it was over. He was dead.*

One by one, the crowd retreated from the room. The images, as swirling and chaotic as they were, are etched in my memory. They don't appear to me as often now, but as I began to contemplate my own end (you see, yet again I have found a way to avoid the word death) and take on the challenge of preparing my advance directive, they resurfaced. I was afraid—for me, for my children, for my grandchildren. I don't want them to feel guilty about letting me go. I think it's my responsibility not to leave them with a lot of unanswered questions and upsetting decisions. I want to make life easier for everyone at a time when there will be enough stress as it is.

Many individuals in my study had been involved in situations in which they had to make a difficult decision about whether or not life-sustaining treatment should be initiated, continued, or discontinued for a family member, most often a parent or spouse. In those situations where there had been no previous discussions about end-of-life, several indicated that they still feel guilty about the decisions that they made. One participant recalled how she and her brother consented to invasive brain surgery for their frail 94-year-old mother, even though they had doubts about whether this was the right course of action. Many years later, the daughter still harbours feelings of guilt.

Another participant, whose husband died of cancer, had a very different experience. She and her husband had prepared directives, and when he was no longer able to make decisions for himself, she and her family members found it reassuring to return to the directive for guidance whenever a treatment decision was being made. If the treatment was compatible with the goals he had outlined and the family had discussed, it was initiated. If the treatment was not compatible, it was withheld. As her husband's condition continued to deteriorate, decisions about such treatments as tube feedings, blood transfusions, medications, and oxygen all had to be made. Making these sorts of decisions was still difficult, and the ultimate outcome of death was overwhelmingly sad, but feelings of guilt seemed much less evident. Indeed, this participant indicated that the family was very comfortable with the decision-making process and the outcomes.

Why then is the decision to withhold treatment for a loved one, especially a treatment that is not likely to be beneficial, and may be potentially harmful, so difficult for many? Given that everyone dies, why are we so often ill-equipped to deal with it when it happens to someone we know and love? Simone de Beauvoir's thoughts about her mother's death reflect how much easier it is to consider a stranger's aging and death than that of a loved one. She says, "'He is certainly of an age to die'…I too made use of this cliché…I did not understand that one might sincerely weep for a relative, a grandfather aged seventy and more. If I met a woman of fifty overcome with sadness because she had just lost her mother, I thought her neurotic: we are all mortal; at eighty you are quite old enough to be one of the dead" (de Beauvoir, 1965, p. 105).

Alice describes feeling helpless as she stood trapped in the corner of the hospital room and watched her husband die. To be helpless is to be unable to function independently or act without help, unable to aid, assist, or provide a person with what is needed or sought (Barber, 2001). Earlier, Alice recounted her experience as a young child seeing her mother's pain, but being unable to provide comfort or relief. These experiences left their mark on Alice emotionally and physically. She does not want her children to have a similar experience with their own mother's death, her death. Protecting her children and grandchildren from the experience of helplessness is equally, if not even more, important to Alice than protecting herself from pain and suffering. This notion of protecting others, of keeping them safe from harm, was very strong in the participants' stories. One participant resolutely told me, "You know, they lost their father to cancer. And they watched him die by inches…and…(sighs) it took him a very long time to die and it was really so painful for my kids that it was just like they were being pulled through a keyhole. And when I first got my first cancer I was so angry I said, 'I am not going to put my children through that again.'"

This feeling of helplessness is also reflected in popular literature. Mitch Albom (1997) recounts his first encounter with death, that of a close family member, this way. He says, "My favorite uncle, my mother's brother, the man who had taught me music, taught me to drive, teased me about girls, thrown me a football—that one adult whom I targeted as a child and said, 'That's who I want to be when I grow up'—died of pancreatic cancer at the age of forty-four. He was a short, handsome man with a thick mustache, and I was with him for the last year of his life, living in an apartment just below his. I watched his strong body wither, then bloat, saw him suffer, night after night, doubled over at the dinner table, pressing on his stomach, his eyes shut, his mouth contorted in pain. 'Ahhhhh, God,' he would moan. 'Ahhhhh, Jesus!' The rest of us—my aunt, his two young sons, me—stood there, silently, cleaning the plates, averting our eyes. It was the most helpless I have ever felt in my life" (pp. 14–15).

Burden is a notion that frequently enters into discussions around end-of-life decision-making. There is a general belief reflected in these stories and the literature that preparing an advance directive will ease the burden of end-of-life decision-making for family members and healthcare providers (Backlar & McFarland, 1996; Beauchamp & Childress, 1994; Colvin, Myhre, Welch, & Hammes, 1993; Downie, 1992; Kelley, 1995; Kuhse, 1999; Mendelssohn & Singer, 1994; Singer, 1995). But what is meant by this concept of burden? Why are end-of-life decisions considered burdensome? How does preparing a directive decrease the burden?

In the dictionary, burden is defined as "something difficult to bear physically or emotionally" (Webster, 1984, p. 97). It seems to follow that making decisions about life-sustaining treatment is potentially difficult for several reasons. Perhaps the most compelling factor is their finality. If one makes the decision to shut off the ventilator that is keeping a loved one alive, the outcome is most likely death. There is no opportunity to go back and make a different decision, to have a second chance to get it right. End-of-life decisions are also difficult to make because they potentially sever long-standing, loving relationships. Deciding not to initiate artificial nutrition and hydration for your mother, the one who nourished you, can be emotionally heart wrenching.

It seems readily apparent that making end-of-life decisions is burdensome. But the question remains—how does preparing a directive diminish the burden? Will having discussions about "pulling the plug" with trusted family and friends make it easier to do so when the time comes? Will knowing that this is what their much-loved friend or relative wanted reduce the emotional pain of losing them, the guilt of making a decision in which the only predictable outcome is death? I think the answer is a cautious yes. If I was the appointed decision-maker for a family or friend, I think I would find it helpful to be able to say to myself, "I am doing what she wanted. I am fulfilling her wishes." Although the burden may not be eliminated, I can imagine how this might be a healing thought to carry forward in my own life. The stories that participants shared with me reaffirmed this belief.

In the literature, burden is discussed most often in relation to the decision-making process itself, rather than in terms of the witness feeling helpless in the face of another's suffering. Is there a way that healthcare providers can do more to assist family members to feel helpful, needed? Can healthcare professionals provide family members with the knowledge, resources, and space they need to help their loved ones? Can they do better at supporting and guiding families through the dying process? Are there times when the healthcare professional's role might be to shield families from witnessing some of the most horrific situations? Perhaps someone should have removed Alice from her husband's room; at least someone could have stood with her, alongside her, and helped her make sense of what was happening. There are no right or wrong answers, no prescriptive care maps that tell healthcare professionals what to do next in these sorts of end-of-life situations. However, if a satisfactory outcome is to be achieved, healthcare professionals must be continuously attentive and attuned to everyone involved.

controlling technology

A week after the information session, at one of our regular Wednesday lunches, I mentioned to my girlfriends that I was going to complete an advance directive. The first question one of them asked me was, "Why?" I started to rattle off some reasons the lawyer had shared with us. "Well, first of all," I told them, "I want to have some say in what happens to me. I don't want my life to continue if I am in severe pain or comatose with no reasonable hope of recovery. Second, I don't want my children to be forced to tell the doctors to pull the plug on their mother. That would be an awful position to put them in. Once I've got it written down, they can feel more comfortable that they are following their mother's wishes. They'll know it is acceptable. That it is truly what I want done."

I paused for a moment and then added some things that the lawyer hadn't mentioned. "You see," I said, "I have many reservations about the medical profession. I've seen first hand some of the things that they do in the name of the Hippocratic oath or whatever. There are times when they don't know when to stop. They seem to have a hard time recognizing when enough is enough. I know it's their training to save lives, but I've lived a good life. It's okay for them to let me go. It is my hope and desire that by completing my own directive I will be allowed to die peacefully and comfortably."

By preparing a directive, the study participants are attempting to protect themselves from the actions of healthcare professionals, from technology, and from pain and suffering. They are also seeking to protect others (family, healthcare professionals, society) from being burdened with making difficult end-of-life decisions, from shouldering expenses related to unwanted life-sustaining treatments, and from the feelings of helplessness that may accompany witnessing an individual's pain and suffering. One of the most enduring tenets of the Hippocratic oath is to do no harm. Although the intentions of healthcare professionals may have been good, the older adults in my study had experiences in which they interpreted the actions of health professionals as detrimental or harmful. Alice's story is not unique. Without exception, everyone I talked with had seen others, most often close family members, suffer at the end-of-life at the hands of healthcare professionals. Some told stories of unnecessary invasive surgeries being performed. Others talked about indignities family members experienced in their interactions with health professionals. Still others told anecdotes about family members whose lives were forever changed when resuscitative measures were used against their wishes and the patients sustained significant brain injuries from which they never recovered. One participant, in describing the care his elderly mother-in-law received, said, "All she wanted to do was just go to sleep and die, but they [the healthcare providers] wouldn't allow it—they forced that poor woman up every day and she was absolutely beside herself...I don't want that happening to me…maybe that's a selfish thing, but that helped me decide to go ahead with the directive."

In retrospect, researchers involved in the SUPPORT study, a national study about end-of-life care and advance directives in the United States, recognized that in designing their study "a crucial fact was underappreciated: advance directives rest on mistrust based on a history of overtreatment from physician paternalism" (Prendergast, 2001, p. 36). How did this history of overtreatment arise? When did this adversarial relationship between patients and healthcare professionals begin? What has happened to the image of the doctor or nurse at the bedside, holding the patient's hand, stroking her forehead, quietly supporting her through the dying process? Is there a way for healthcare professionals to value death in the same way they value life, rather than to view the two as mutually exclusive?

Life-sustaining treatments like ventilators, tube feedings, cardiopulmonary resuscitation, and organ transplantation are all costly procedures. Through their own experiences with family members, through television and news reports, and through the popular media, participants in my study were aware of the many technological advances in the medical field. They believed that life could be sustained almost indefinitely if the arsenal of weapons available to the healthcare team was fully deployed. These older adults were adamant that they did not want to receive life-sustaining treatments if they were terminally ill or had little chance of recovering to their previous state of health. One participant said, "I don't want to waste taxpayers' dollars by keeping me alive just for somebody's…ego or something." By limiting what they perceived to be unnecessary treatments at the end-of-life, these individuals hoped that financial savings would be recognized by their families and society at large, and that this money would be used to improve the lives of others.

It has been hypothesized that advance directives reduce costs at the end-of-life through the withholding of expensive life-sustaining treatments (Sansone & Phillips, 1995). Several studies that have examined cost implications associated with the implementation of advance directives have found negligible cost savings (Fins, 1997; Perrin, 1997). Yet others have found considerable cost savings (Molloy et al., 2000). Cost-benefit analyses of this type are very complex and the conflicting findings of these studies are difficult to interpret

(Ott, 1999). Common sense, however, would suggest that withdrawal of life-sustaining treatment would be less costly than continued application of expensive technologies. Although cost factors should not be the driving force behind end-of-life decisions, given the current economic climate and the reality that healthcare resources are not unlimited, it is appropriate that costs be given some consideration at the societal level.

It seems ironic to consider that life-saving technologies developed to benefit humanity and to support life, such as cardiopulmonary resuscitation, have become the enemy in situations where death is imminent. At one time, these technologies were applied very narrowly to certain types of patient conditions, specifically a sudden and unexpected cardiac or respiratory arrest. Over the past few decades, however, their use has become much more generalized. In their book entitled *Final Passages*, Ahronheim and Weber (1992) suggest that "we fear the unchecked growth of technology and the loss of a personal connection between ourselves and our caregivers... We no longer believe in the idea of a social safety net that will catch us or a morally responsible community watching over and protecting our interests. We feel somewhat abandoned" (p. 14).

How has it come to be that technology has not only entered the room of the dying, but it has taken over and invaded the space? Why has the social safety net disappeared? In preparing their directives, Alice and others like her are attempting to control the amount, timing, and types of technology that will be allowed to enter into their private sphere as they approach death. When used at the bedside, however, one wonders if advance directives might be looked upon as just another tool, an instrument that dictates care from afar and is disassociated from the individual lying in the bed. In my current work as a clinical ethicist, I received a call from a staff member who was concerned about the treatment a patient was receiving. She indicated that the patient had arrived from another facility with a feeding tube in place that was contrary to what was written in her advance directive. Her question to me was, "Should we take it out?" My question to her was, "Is the patient capable?" Her response was, "Yes." I suggested she discuss the feeding tube situation with the patient. As it turns out, the patient had a cancer that was impeding her ability to swallow safely. Since she was still feeling relatively well and was not imminently dying, she had consented to the feeding tube as a way of maintaining her nutritional status.

Anecdotally, I have heard of other situations where the written instructions in an advance directive seemed to take precedent over the wishes of a capable individual, perhaps because directives have status as recognized legal documents. If not used appropriately, is it possible that advance directives could become just another piece of technology—another interference in the dying process, another tool that distances care providers from their patients? To prevent such a situation, healthcare providers need to stay focussed on the provider/ patient relationship. It is worth restating here that advance directives come into effect only after the patient is found to be incapable of making treatment decisions.

fostering family relationships

I went on to tell my girlfriends the story of Mr. S., whose children were in conflict about whether or not his pneumonia should be treated. My children are very independent, and they have divergent views on a lot of topics: Christine's into a lot of New Age stuff—alternative medicine and the like—while Susan and David are more conservative. It's not that difficult for me to imagine a scene as they gather around my deathbed—Susan insisting that treatment be stopped, Christine saying there are alternative therapies that might help, and David, always the mediator, trying to help the two reach some compromise. Then there are the sons- and daughter-in-law and my grandchildren. You know the phrase, "Too many cooks spoil the broth"? Well, I think the same thing could happen here if I don't do something to prevent it. Too many people, all with the best of intentions, trying to direct my care—a recipe for potential disaster!

By writing out what I want, and who I want to make the decisions, I hope to prevent disagreements and hard feelings among my children. I don't want my death to be divisive. I want my children to remain close when I am gone. I want them to have good relationships with each other.

Initially, I thought preparing an advance directive was a solitary activity undertaken to ensure that what an individual wanted to happen actually did. As my conversations with older adults continued, it became apparent that maintaining good familial relationships was a critical reason for completing a directive. One participant said,

"This way it's all there, there is no argument and, yeah, this is the way Mom wants it, and they go along, right there and then. Because I want them to continue to be friends. They can argue about the colour of the paint on the wall or something else, but the big things shouldn't have to be [argued about]." Another said, "I have a responsibility to my loved ones not to leave them with a lot of unanswered questions and a lot of decisions that upset some and don't upset others, and I believe that it is my job to make sure that they continue to be friends." Still another said it was her intent "to try and alleviate the children not speaking to each other because each one wants something different." Preserving family connections was as important to these older adults as protecting themselves from pain and suffering. They viewed this as a lasting legacy in which they could play a pivotal role. Advance directives were perceived to be a vehicle that supported this goal.

preserving one's identity

Something I hadn't realized until I attended the information session was that a directive can include directions about more than just healthcare, like where I want to live and with whom I want to associate. I had to consider questions like: Who am I? What are my defining features? What makes me, me? What do I really value in life?

Hmm. A few ideas about the things that are important to me come immediately to mind. I want to stay living in my own home as long as possible. I wouldn't say I am a materialistic person, but I am pretty attached to some of my things—my collection of Native artwork, my perfectly-stuffed reading chair, my photo albums, my curio cabinet bursting at the seams with mementoes from my travels. If I need to go to a nursing home, please don't let them play country music on the radio in my room. And I hate purple—so when I am old, I ask that you not dress me in purple or a red hat. You may have guessed by now that I love to talk, and read, and talk, and listen, and talk. It is my life's passion. If I can't talk, if I can't engage in a conversation with those around me, I might as well be dead. And of course, there's my family, they're the most important of all. No matter what, I want them to be close by.

Making an advance directive is perceived as a way of extending one's personhood into a future time of diminished capacity. Personhood is the quality or condition of being an individual person (Barber, 2001). Alice has described some of the things that make Alice, Alice. Some of what she identifies, like the music she abhors, may seem rather trivial in the context of a life and death discussion. Yet if you were subjected to listening to a style of music that you disliked every day, all day, for weeks or months on end, it might be an unusual kind of torture and certainly would impact your overall quality of life.

Historically, as discussed earlier, one of the main arguments against the use of advance directives centres on the notion of personhood (Degrazia, 1999; de Raeve, 1993; Downie, 1992; Kuhse, 1999; May, 1997; Mendelssohn & Singer, 1994; Tonelli, 1996). This line of reasoning plays out in two contrasting ways. One line of reasoning concludes that an individual who is now incompetent is no longer the same person, and so, any directive prepared while competent ought not to have moral authority in the current situation (Degrazia, 1999; de Raeve, 1993; Mendelssohn & Singer, 1994). While this may in some ways be true, I would argue that there is still some ongoing connection to the previous person and that what has been written in an advance directive may be the closest representation of the person's wishes that we are able to access.

The second argument goes even further and concludes that an incompetent individual no longer meets the criteria of personhood and is thus a non-person (Kuhse, 1999). As a non-person, any connection to the person who wrote the advance directive is severed, and the document's contents are declared illegitimate. As a non-person, the incompetent individual is deemed to have no right to receive life-sustaining treatment (Kuhse, 1999).

Although these two arguments about the notion of personhood may be philosophically sound, they seem to be of limited value at the bedside when an end-of-life decision must be made for a specific individual. They seem to rely upon a conception of person and body as distinct entities (Emanuel, 1995). As a nurse who has cared for individuals both before and after an incapacitating event (such as a stroke), I do not find that the non-person argument fits well with the realities of healthcare. It is difficult to accept that the individual I cared for yesterday is a person, and today, because of a catastrophic event that happened overnight, is no longer a person but rather a body. If it were only a body lying in the bed, not a person worthy of care and attention, I would not be called or required to act. Yet, in my experience in such situations, I am called to act in an ethical manner that strives to do exactly the opposite of separating person and body. In providing care, I am seeking to preserve the personhood and dignity of the individual to the greatest extent possible.

For me, it seems reasonable to imagine that some vestiges of the person are likely to continue to be present across time and incompetence. I wonder if healthcare professionals have paid enough attention to the concept of personhood. They take complicated medical histories, they know everything about a patient's body parts, inside and out, but how often do they get to know the person as an individual (Bergum & Dossetor, 2005)? Entering into a dialogue with patients about their advance directives may be one way of gaining insight into who they are as a person. As Hatfield and McHutchion (1993) suggest, "The most useful part of a document like that [an advance directive] is to get the discussion started...For that's its greatest value. It is a voice for the silent and protection for the incompetent, but also a prompt for the competent" (p. 33).

In describing when they would no longer want to receive life-sustaining treatment, participants focussed on the notion of quality of life. Their discussions on quality of life primarily focussed on three areas: independence, being able to communicate, and familiar people and surroundings. One participant stated, "It's important to me that I'm able to feed myself, that I can still read, talk, watch television, or do just the things that I do today, maybe not quite as well as I do them now." Another expressed a similar sentiment when he said, "I don't want my family to have to sit me in a chair and have to feed me gruel all the rest of my life. I want a quality of life." For another individual, being able to get around independently was important, but she thought that "the most difficult to deal with [would be] if you couldn't communicate." Reinforcing this notion of the importance of communication, another participant said even more forcefully, "If they know that I can't speak, I don't want to wake up and find out I can't speak. If I can't speak, don't plug me in the channel." For this participant, life without the ability to communicate was not perceived as worth living. Do healthcare providers know what their patients consider to be important to their quality of life? How do we, ourselves, define quality of life?

Two participants had lived through the experience of caring for their husbands at home during the dying process. They both spoke of the importance of familiar people and surroundings, and how it had affected not only their husbands but also themselves and other family members. One stated, "I was able to bring him home and I know he didn't want to go in a strange room with strangers, and I know that every day that he was alive and awake he was happy to be home." The other said, "There were people who thought we were a little crazy having him home, but for us it was the right thing to do...At the time, three of the kids had young children. They could bring them here whereas you couldn't in the hospital...My youngest daughter had a baby amidst all of this, who lived in the laundry basket at the foot of her grandpa's bed." These women also felt they were better able to control what was happening to their loved one than if he were in the hospital. One talked specifically about being able to provide her husband with pain medication on a regular schedule and on time, something that had not happened when he was hospitalized because staff were busy and unpredictable events repeatedly interrupted the delivery of care. How can healthcare providers ensure that space, whether the patient is at home, in hospital, or in another setting, is made in the dying process for family members and familiar surroundings? Fortunately, in Canada today, there are several options available for most persons who are dying to receive palliative care at home, in hospices, or in hospital. The right option for each individual may vary for many reasons.

As the opening quotation from de Beauvoir reminds us, it is unfortunate that healthcare providers have come to be seen as persons to compete against. (She calls the physician a "dangerous opponent" because of his ability to keep a patient alive despite the patient's acceptance of death.) In many ways, it is this perception of healthcare providers that has stimulated a number of individuals, including the older adults who participated in my study, to complete advance directives. Ultimately, if end-of-life care is to be improved, it would seem that this competitive stance must be replaced with one that values relationships instead. Developing relationships with our fellow human beings in a respectful, open, and responsive manner is of utmost importance throughout life, from birth to death, and a goal that is most worthy of pursuit. To be successful in optimizing the experience of death for every individual, healthcare professionals, patients, and family members must work together to protect ourselves and others.

facing
ONE'S MORTALITY

2

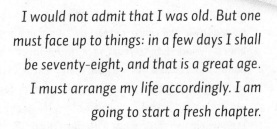

I would not admit that I was old. But one must face up to things: in a few days I shall be seventy-eight, and that is a great age. I must arrange my life accordingly. I am going to start a fresh chapter.

(de Beauvoir, 1965, p. 17)

meeting death

I can clearly recall the first time I became aware of the fact that one day I would die. When my own mother died, I was too young to comprehend the full meaning of death, and I don't remember making any connection between her death and my own mortality. It was a number of years later that death stared me squarely in the face—that I saw myself, dead. I was sitting in the front pew at a funeral home chapel, awaiting the beginning of my grandmother's service. I was 22 years old, newly married, and expecting my first child. I remember squeezing my husband's hand so firmly that he turned to me and whispered tersely, "Alice, loosen the grip. I can't feel my fingers." More than 50 years later, the layout of the room at the funeral home is easy to describe. In front of me, a little to the left, is a lectern standing at attention. There are green velvet chairs with walnut-stained arms arranged in small groupings along the edge of the room. Flowers are everywhere, vibrant colours with shiny ribbons proclaiming the relationship of the giver to the deceased—mother, grandmother, sister. There is a certain smell, too, somewhat sweet but not quite floral, gentle and calming yet difficult to identify.

While I sat there quietly on the hard wooden bench, the baby growing inside me kicked—a hard kick, high up in my belly—and kicked again. The contrast between my baby's vigorous movements and my grandmother's motionless body was striking. The circle of life and death was in me and around me, near me and beyond me, tangible yet elusive. For a fleeting moment, I saw myself lying in the coffin. I knew at that moment that, one day, I too would die. I silently wondered what lay beyond mortal death *for my grandmother, for me, for my child. Was my grandmother looking in on us here, right now? Would the time come when we were all united once again, together forever? I hoped so. I believed so. To think otherwise was beyond comprehension, too frightening. As I set out to complete my advance directive, these memories surfaced into consciousness. In the process, I was forced to come face to face with my own mortality once again, and to make every attempt to accept it with grace and humility.*

Alice's first vivid memory of facing her own mortality evoked a powerful and long-lasting effect. For the participants in the study I conducted, completing their directive seemed to involve facing and accepting their own mortality. Many authors, both in the scientific and fictional literature, have written about the significance of this event. In the context of my conversations with older adults, several shared their first remembrances of confronting their own mortality. One participant told her story this way: "As a child I had a very bad accident and they were not able to do anything about it medically speaking. I'm now 81 and it happened when I was 4. From that time on, I had the wish to have my body turned over to the medical schools so that they could find a way to heal what had been my problem. And so this is my first recollection of me thinking about what would happen when I die."

Implicitly, I was both challenged and encouraged by the participants' stories to reflect upon my own experiences with death. Growing up on a farm, the death of animals and pets was a fairly regular occurrence in my youth. Yet as there was always another puppy or kitten or pig that quickly replaced the one that died, I do not think those experiences evoked for me questions about mortality, my own or others'. When I was ten, though, my grandmother died and I was forced to confront death in a different way. Soon after my tenth birthday, my grandmother became seriously ill and was hospitalized. When it became evident that she was not going to survive her illness, my parents gathered my brothers and sister and me up, dressed in our Sunday finest, and we drove the ten or so miles to the local small-town hospital to visit my grandmother. Although I don't remember my parents telling us that Grandma was dying, I somehow knew. Maybe it was the expression on my parents' faces as they exchanged fleeting glances. Maybe it was the stillness in the cool autumn air. I don't know how, but I had a feeling this would be the last time I would see my grandma alive.

Hospitals at this time had strict rules about visitation, one of them being that no children were allowed under any circumstances. Leaving my mom, my brothers, sister, and me in the car, my dad strode with confident steps towards the front doors of the hospital to ask the staff if perhaps the rules could be bent this one time. After we waited for what seemed like forever, we spotted him through the entrance door windows. We knew by his slumped shoulders that our request had not been granted. He told us that the nurses were going to move my grandma's bed close to the window in her room so that she could see us and we could wave to her. My father then got into the car and drove it to the back of the building, bringing it to a stop beneath my grandma's hospital room. We got out and stood beside the car, gazing up in the direction of my father's pointed finger. My grandmother's silhouette is emblazoned in my mind. I see the second floor window with its white metal frame surrounded by golden yellow bricks. I see a nurse with her stiff-peaked cap behind my grandma, supporting her as she leans toward the window to wave to us. And I feel the tears stream down my cheeks as I silently wave back. I feel her love and her wisdom, too. In this moment, I know that my grandma will always be with me—that neither windows nor walls nor death will separate our spirits.

Sometime later at the funeral home, I remember sitting by myself on one of the couches along the edge of the room and a cousin my same age coming and asking me why I was crying. Wasn't it obvious? I thought. Didn't she understand? Grandma was dead and she wasn't coming back. Didn't she know there would be no more taste-testing of her oatmeal cookie batter, no more playing cards with her at the kitchen table? Grandpa would be all alone in their big farm house. It was a brutal awakening for me, and the emotions are still powerful today. A box of tissue sits nearby as I write this. I wonder if the introduction to death, that first encounter, can ever be gentle. I wonder if there is an easier way to meet death. I wonder why my cousin did not seem as upset as I was. And I wonder how one's first experiences with death shape one's later beliefs and attitudes about death and dying. Brookes (1997) proposes that "understanding death involves an inward as well as an outward journey" (p. 39). Of your first death experience he states that you should consider the following: "What was its tone? Its color? What connotations and denotations did it suggest for the word *death* that to this day affect the way you shape the word in your mouth, the expression on your face, the slope of your shoulders as you say it?" (Brookes, 1997, p. 39). In response to his queries, I say it out loud—death—and I feel how it rolls off my tongue; I feel my eyes squint together and my brows furrow. I try smiling as I speak the word death. It feels awkward, unnatural, not at all right.

interacting with death

Now that I am in my golden years, my interactions with death come more often and more closely together. Recently, I attended five funerals in four weeks—funerals of long-time friends and family members. My turn is coming one day. I can't say that I'm looking forward to it. I still have a list of things I'd like to accomplish, but I'm not afraid. You may not believe me, but I have no fear of death. I see it as life's next great adventure. Forgive me if I am repeating myself, but this is an important point that I want to make sure you understand. I firmly believe that there's something beyond, that death isn't the end but only another beginning. I think that we go to a different level, exactly where it is I am not sure. It will be a time when I am reunited with family and friends who have gone before me. It will be a time when I am pain free, worry free. No longer will I have to be concerned about whether I will outlive my pension, whether it will rain or snow tomorrow, whether the car will start when I turn the key in the ignition. All of these earthly worries will be irrelevant. My father once told me, "You can have anything you want. You can do anything you want. But you can wear only one pair of shoes at a time." I think he was trying to tell me that life isn't about power, fame, fortune, or wealth; it's about living each day to its fullest without regrets.

It's unfortunate that in our hustle and bustle society, we don't take the time to be quiet, to be introspective, to think about what's really important. I've come to appreciate the time that I've spent contemplating how I've lived my life as I prepared my directive. Having a specific project, a specific goal in mind, forced me to take that time.

One of the realities that accompany aging is the loss of family members and friends through death. If an individual comes from a large family as I do, I can only imagine what it must be like to watch one's siblings die, one by one. To be the last alive ought, I suppose, to be a triumph, but I suspect it to be a hollow one. To attend five funerals in a month, as Alice describes, would be, I imagine, emotionally draining, almost unbearable. Yet, she seems to take it all in stride. One study participant who had also attended a number of funerals reflected on his experience this way: "We've been to a lot of funerals lately and some of the people who are gone were just tremendous people. In fact, one of them, the service was an hour long, which is awfully long for a funeral. But it almost took that length of time to spell out and give an example of all the things the man had done and accomplished in his life. So you sit there and squirm a little bit and think, man, what have I done with my life? What would people say at my funeral?"

In experiencing and interacting with death and illness while preparing her own advance directive, another participant described being compelled to think about her own mortality. In responding to my question, "Did going through the process of completing your directive make you think about your own mortality?" she said, "Ah, very much so, very much. Like my husband was healthy, we thought, the cancer was found accidentally on his lung. How quickly things can change. I also have a brother, he's ten years younger than I am and he had a stroke! And we can't, even four or five years later, understand him when he talks. So I knew that I'm the one left here. After my husband passed away, I'm even more aware of it [her mortality], because I'm the one left for my children. So I try and keep a lot of things, you know, very organized because there's a lot of trauma without it." Alongside an acknowledgement of her own mortality, she has a desire to make things easier for those left behind and believes that an advance directive will assist in this way. For many of the participants, being exposed to death within their inner circle of family and friends seems to be an important part of coming face to face with their own mortality.

Another study participant recounted an experience that changed her entire outlook on death and dying. She attended an interactive workshop a number of years ago on death and dying. She participated in an exercise in which the facilitator took attendees on a guided imagery trip. The facilitator encouraged the participants to imagine their own deaths, beginning with their doctor telling them, "You have a fatal disease and you are going to die." He asked them to envision saying goodbye to three people that they knew and loved, and then he took them to a tunnel. He suggested that participants take one person with them for part of the journey, but she chose to go alone. She didn't want to have to say goodbye again. He told them they would be given a word or a phrase as they entered the tunnel. The phrase she saw come down from the ceiling of the tunnel was "I AM." At the end of this tunnel she saw a man in a long white robe and a beard, and he had his hand out in a welcoming gesture. For this woman, the experience was reassuring and alleviated many of the fears she had about dying. At the time of the workshop she described herself as an atheist. Although she did not share with me the meaning that the words "I am" held for her, the message I took away was that it is enough to be, to exist, that nothing more is asked or required of us.

Not everyone will have had an experience with imagery like this participant, yet many reach an analogous conclusion. Scott-Maxwell (1968) frames her approach to the end-of-life as a time of discovery. She says, "A *long life* makes me feel nearer truth, yet it won't go into words, so how can I convey it? I can't, and I want to. I want to tell people approaching and perhaps fearing age that it is a time of discovery. If they say—'Of what?' I can only answer, 'We must each find out for ourselves, otherwise it won't be discovery.' I want to say—'If at the end of your life you have only yourself, it is much. Look, you will find'" (Scott-Maxwell, 1968, p. 142). I wonder how many of us, regardless of our age, take the time to look inside, to seek our own inner truths, to consider what our own process of discovery might reveal.

It has been said, "All religions unequivocally believe in some sort of life or state of being after death" (Anderson, 2001, p. 74). Alice describes this phase as a great adventure. The use of the term "adventure" surfaced in several of my conversations with study participants. One participant said, somewhat apologetically, "I think that the greatest adventure of life is dying and that may sound hokey or something. But birth and death are remarkable things." Similarly, another said, "It [death] seems like it might be an exciting adventure." In speaking of her mother's death, de Beauvoir (1965) also refers to adventure when she writes, "We were taking part in the dress rehearsal for our own burial. The misfortune is that although everyone must come to this, each experiences the adventure in solitude. We never left Maman during those last days which she confused with convalescence and yet we were profoundly separated from her" (pp. 99–100). Gadamer (1982) states that "an adventure, interrupts the customary course of events, but is positively and significantly related to the context which it interrupts—thus an adventure lets life become felt as a whole, in its breadth and in its strength—here lies the fascination of an adventure. It removes the conditions and obligations of everyday life. It ventures out into the uncertain" (p. 62). Death seems to fit this description of adventure well. It is an interruption in life's flow and takes one into the vast unknown.

Conceptualizing death as an adventure, however, is somewhat problematic for me because we usually think of an adventure as something one must live through to tell the tale. Although there have been near-death stories recounted in the literature, to date no one has ever returned to tell us about death in all its fullness. Even when we are in death's presence, as de Beauvoir reminds us, we are still distant from it. Will we ever come closer to knowing death and what lies beyond? Or is it perhaps one of life's mysteries that is best left unknown?

Most participants had spent some time thinking about how they would want their own death to unfold. One said, "I wouldn't want to linger on for a long, long time, you know. I think I'd rather go kind of quickly, maybe not too quickly, cause that's a shock for people. But by the same token, I wouldn't mind just sort of dropping dead though, or going, dying, in my sleep or something like that." A desire to die in one's sleep was frequently expressed. "I actually hope that I can die in my sleep with a heart attack or something. That would be so nice," said one participant. Echoing this sentiment, another said, "I'm just hoping that I will go to bed one night and my heart will stop." By dying in one's sleep, is one hoping to somehow miss the event? When people lie down to sleep at night, do they consider the possibility that they will not wake? A prayer I recall from my childhood does just that.

> Now I lay me down to sleep,
> I pray the Lord my soul to keep.
> If I should die before I wake,
> I pray the Lord my soul to take.

Is imagining how one would prefer to die a useful exercise? Or is it an exercise in futility?

Participants in my study seem to have found a way to interact with death that for most was manageable, rather than disabling or depressing. How they have achieved this equilibrium remains hidden. Perhaps the alternative is simply too difficult to sustain. Muriel Spark (as cited by Anderson, 2001) offers the following insight: "If I had my life to live over again, I would form the habit of nightly composing myself to thoughts of death. I would practice, as it were, the remembrance of death. There is not another practice which so intensifies life. Death, when it approaches, ought not to take one by surprise. It should be part of the full expectancy of life" (p. 21). Maybe it is only by turning our attention to death and incorporating it into our daily practices that we can become more comfortable and accepting of its inevitability.

accepting death

If you were to ask me if I have accepted death, I would probably answer yes…and no. Maybe it's because of my background, my life experiences— I've personally witnessed two people die, my mother and my husband, and some other fairly tragic things have happened to family and friends over the years. I wouldn't say I'm callous or that I've got a thick skin, but life brings what it brings, and the end of it is inevitable whether you live 40, 60, or 100 years. It's still just a snap of a finger in time in comparison to eternity. If it were up to me, I would like a few more years to see my grandchildren grow up, to see who they become as adults, maybe even to see my great-grandchildren begin their life journeys. Just imagine the things they will do and see in their lifetimes—it boggles the mind. To think that a part of me, well, at least some of my genes, will live on through them—it's quite remarkable. Perhaps one of my descendants will live on the moon, or discover the cure for cancer, or travel virtually around the world without ever leaving home. Yet, if my time were up tomorrow, that would be okay, too. I'm prepared for death. I've talked with my family. To the best of my knowledge there aren't any unresolved issues. As I've said before, I'm not afraid of death or of what comes after it.

In my conversations with study participants, I was struck by their overall sense of acceptance of death and their general lack of fear of death and what lies beyond. At times this was related to an individual's faith or religious convictions about the existence of an after world. For others, the notion of a life after death was not as important. One man told me, "I've lived a fairly good period of time now, but I really haven't contributed very much except carbon dioxide. So it'll be no great loss to me. I won't know about it anyway." He went on further to say, "There's no fear at all at this point. No, the only thing, to me, it's like when I left home, like I say when I was 17 years old...you're a kid. You don't know a lot of what waits for you when you get where you're going...and this is the same thing. It's more of leaving this behind than going some place else. Because after 71 years, you know you're used to this and you don't know what you're getting next."

Another woman said, "I think my life step-by-step as it has unfolded has been acceptable to me and pleasurable enough and when it ends it ends. There are very few really, really strong wishes or convictions that I've had that would make me want to live over and above the years that I am now. I mean, I always, I shouldn't say always, but at least from the time I was 70 I felt, 'Ah! I could die any old day now. I've done nearly all the things that I want to do,' and the things that I haven't been able to do are just a matter of time, but they are not that important that I want to live in pain or live with wires and, you know, machines. I would much rather be gone and be remembered as a person that had a real spark of life and it's gone. And the older I get, the more I feel that way, definitely! I certainly don't want to be hooked up in any hospital bed, not even overnight! Don't even mention it to me (laughs)! That is NOT how I want my life to end (laughs), and I think considering all the nice things they say about you when you're dead, you know, I don't mind (laughs). It [death] can happen any time now while everybody still has a good opinion of me (laughs) and, you know, remembers me as being an active person with all my faculties and foibles and all the rest of it."

Similar descriptions of older adults' attitudes around death and dying exist in the literature. Florence Scott-Maxwell at 83 years of age describes her beliefs and fears about death as follows. "*My only fear about death is that it will not come soon enough. Life still interests and occupies me. Happily I am not in such discomfort that I wish for death, I love and am loved, but please God I die before I lose my independence. I do not know what I believe about life after death;*

if it exists then I burn with interest, if not—well, I am tired. I have endured the flame of living and that should be enough" (Scott-Maxwell, 1968, p. 75). In the novel *As We Are Now*, the extraordinary story of an old woman who is planning her suicide is told. After she decides to commit suicide, she says, "It is strange that now I have made my decision I can prepare for death in a wholly new way. I feel free, beyond attachment, beyond the human world at last. I rejoice as if I were newborn, seeing with wide-open eyes, as only the old can (for the newborn infant cannot see) the marvels of the world" (Sarton, 1973, p. 125).

Fear of death seems to exist on a continuum. Some older adults express a fear of death. One participant in a study examining why older adults do not complete advance directives was reported as saying, "Every time I start filling out the forms, I cry and stop. It makes it seem like death is coming close" (Winland-Brown, 1998, p. 38). In de Beauvoir's (1965) writing about her mother's death, she recalls the words spoken by her mother's friend. "'I can't understand,' said the bewildered Mademoiselle Vauthier. 'Your mother is so religious and so pious, and yet she is so afraid of death!' Did she not know that saints have died convulsed and shrieking? Besides, Maman was not afraid of either God or the Devil: only of leaving this earth" (p. 91). Does talking about and interacting with death proactively help to dissipate some of the fear, to make it more manageable?

When participants in the study I conducted talked about their thoughts on death, they were remarkably calm. Some were even animated when discussing the possibilities that lie beyond. My own struggle to accept death is fuelled by much more angst. I vacillate between knowing intellectually that I will die and yet harbouring thoughts that I am the exception to the rule—that immortality will somehow be prescribed to me. The words of Alexander Sergeyevich Buturlin, as spoken in 1915, capture much of what I feel. He is attributed as saying, "I know that I shall die soon and my mind is reconciled to it; but when I think that my body will be put into a coffin, that the lid of the coffin will be screwed down and I will be buried under earth, I am horrified. I am well aware that my horror is unreasonable, that I shall not be feeling anything by then, but I cannot overcome this feeling. Sometimes I also have the feeling—and that is also unreasonable—that I shall not die" (Enright, 1983, p. 26). Even the eminent psychiatrist Sigmund Freud is cited as offering a similar account suggesting, "In the unconscious every one of us is convinced of his own immortality" (Enright, 1983, p. 154). How do beliefs about death and dying develop?

How is it that the individuals I talked to have come to acknowledge their own mortality with such quiet assurance, with such a degree of comfort? Or is this assurance a ruse, something they have tricked themselves or been tricked into believing? Is it possible to accept something but still be afraid? William Hazlitt (1778–1830) suggests, "The best cure for the fear of death is to reflect that life has a beginning as well as an end. There was a time when we were not: this gives us no concern—why then should it trouble us that a time will come when we shall cease to be?" (Enright, 1983, p. 31). He makes it sound so easy.

Gaines (1993), in his novel about a young man sentenced to die for a murder he did not commit, says of this man's family and friends: "They must believe [in a God, in a life after death]. They must believe, if only to free the mind, if not the body. Only when the mind is free has the body a chance to be free" (p. 251). Like the friends and family of Gaine's character, I find it impossible to imagine that all that remains after death is nothingness. I have yet to come to any conclusion about what the alternative is, but I hold fast to the belief that there is something. I want the opportunity to be reunited with those who have died before me; I want some assurance that those with physical disabilities on earth have an opportunity to move freely; I want to know that young children who have died have the chance to grow up; I want to believe that there is a way that the wrongs and injustices committed on earth can be righted.

Life experiences, such as those illustrated in Alice's story, seem to have shaped the study participants' opinions of death. One man with severe heart disease laughingly described a conversation he had with his cardiac surgeon before a serious operation. "He [the doctor] suggested that I had only a 10 percent chance to come through it. And so I told him, 'Well, look! If I don't make it I'm not going to know it, and if I do make it you're one hell of a surgeon, so go ahead!'" This same man had been an airforce pilot who was involved in a number of plane crashes; he had been shot down by enemy fire twice; and he had lost several of his best mates during the Korean War. He went on to say, "I often said when I was in the service, 'I might be gone before I'm 50' (laughs)…When I made 50, well, everything I have is a bonus (laughs). But, you know, it's just life experience. There's no traumatic experience that says it's [death is] gonna happen." I wonder about the laughter that is interjected throughout many of the stories that the participants shared with me. Is it genuine or a way of coping with a topic that is too difficult to tackle head on? Is it a way of deflecting feelings of a different kind? Is it a way of keeping death at a safe distance?

Although these individuals profess an acceptance of death and a lack of fear about its arrival, I am still not fully convinced. It seems that there is some conflicting testimony in their words. This ambivalence is captured by Scott-Maxwell (1968) when she was about to undergo a surgical procedure. She says, "Of course I might die, I had heard of the heart giving out under an operation, it was possible, but then I would meet the great mystery. It almost seemed my chance. A mean way of slipping out though, not fair to the surgeon, and I want to be conscious that I am dying. I did not want to die, but I have lived my life—or so I used to feel. Now each extra day is a gift. An extra day in which I may gain some new understanding, see a beauty, feel love, or know the richness of watching my youngest grandson express his every like and dislike with force and sweetness. But all this is the sentience by which I survive, and who knows, it may matter deeply how we end so mysterious a thing as living" (pp. 90–91). It appears that I am not alone in my skepticism. Many years ago, Jean-Jacques Rousseau (1712–1778) was quoted as saying, "He who pretends to look on death without fear lies. All men are afraid of dying, this is the great law of sentient beings, without which the entire human species would soon be destroyed" (Enright, 1983, p. 22). Who am I to believe? Does it matter in the end?

Although the participants generally expressed a lack of fear of death and a state of readiness for death, they did not want their lives to be shortened prematurely. One participant, in reflecting on the content of her directive said, "If you stipulate that you never want to be put on life support, I might get dead quicker than I was supposed to." Another said, "I wouldn't want my life terminated ahead of time if I still had some quality of life." Still another said, "It [stopping life-sustaining treatment] shouldn't be done precipitously. In other words,

it couldn't be that I was just unconscious, so let's pull the plug."
All seem to be saying that decisions about life-sustaining treatment
need to be made thoughtfully, taking into account the context of
the situation.

I wonder why someone would want to continue to live here on
earth, if they thought there was something better to come after
death. I wonder if the words to express our beliefs and attitudes
about death exist in our language. In our conversations, I wanted
to challenge participants on their lack of fear about death. I wanted to
ask them if they truly had no fears, if they were being totally honest
with me. I wanted to know if they were hiding something. But such
probing questions seemed inappropriate, disrespectful—even potentially harmful. What right did I have to question their belief system?
My role as researcher was to seek understanding. I wondered if age,
simply having lived more years and being at a different stage in life,
had something to do with their attitudes and beliefs. Will I think as
they do when I am older? The findings in this area are mixed. When
Winland-Brown (1998) talked with older adults who had not prepared
advance directives, a fear of death emerged as a strong reason for not
completing a directive. It may be that age and living more years influence one's acceptance of death; however, age alone does not seem to
be sufficient for dispelling a fear of death. Perhaps I have not yet lived
enough, have not had enough relevant life experiences, to reach a
level of comfort with thinking about my own death. Maybe it is time,
borrowing de Beauvoir's (1965) words, for me to "start a fresh chapter"
and to think about death anew.

Kavanagh (1972) suggests that beliefs about death and dying are
both personal and important to the dying process. He says, "In short,
we might easily conclude that nobody knows for certain about an
afterlife. Instead, I choose to hold with Kierkegaard that every man
knows for himself within his inner soul. Maybe nobody can ever know
what to believe for anyone besides himself. Near death, true belief
in what you sincerely hold will bring peace and any promise you need
for your future" (p. 218). Although this idea of accepting death is
difficult for some, its pursuit seems to be of value. As Burgess (1993)
suggests, "When we confront our own mortality or assist others to
find meaning in their last days of life, we may gain a new perspective

on what for us is of ultimate importance" (p. 46). It seems important that I struggle on in my attempts to accept my own death.

disappearing death

It seems strange how we, in today's society, try to hide death, to make it disappear. At one time, dead bodies were kept in the homes of their families for days on end and everyone, even small children, came to visit and celebrate the life of the deceased. Now the dead are whisked away to a funeral home. And if you're in hospital, it's sometimes hard to die. Some doctors and nurses don't want to accept death as an outcome—they see death as an enemy, and if it can't be conquered then they have failed. I've had friends who for all intents and purposes were dead, but they were hooked up to machines. They had a heartbeat, they were breathing, but they weren't alive. Nobody would let them die. Yet we see lots of images of death on television, on the news and in TV shows. But somehow these images don't seem real. They don't seem to have much of an impact on us, on the way we live.

Megory Anderson (2001) compares the concept of death to "the elephant [standing] in the living room, while everyone awkwardly discusses the weather" (p. 18). To make an elephant (death) disappear is a trick worthy of a great magician, yet in the last few generations our society seems to have accomplished this with relative ease. How did this happen? Is it a good thing? One participant in describing her own cultural background talked about how "years ago your culture was that you embraced death as a part of life. You know the Old Irish ways where the body was brought into the house, and everybody waked the body in the house and then it went to the church and after that the whole community, your culture, was there to nourish you through that period." Another participant, referring to a notice I placed in a senior's centre about my study, described how he found death was often a taboo topic. He said, "I do notice in the Senior Centre you can't talk about things like that. Your sheet is up there and I've asked some of the guys and they say, 'Oh, I bought it [an advance directive, living will] at Staples and filled it in or I saw a lawyer and he's done it.' And I know they haven't seen a lawyer. And I know when the man's lying and when he isn't, in most cases. And a lot of them say or some of them say, 'Look! I worked all my life, now it's up to her.' And I don't think they really mean that. I think they're scared to sit down and talk with their wife." This participant attributes the silence to fear, and if his assessment is accurate, individuals may sometimes even lie to avoid a conversation about death.

In describing how this avoidance of death has come to pass, Hatfield and McHutchion (1993) suggest that the shift from death in the home to death in the hospital is a defining factor. They state that "in the past two generations we have allowed death to become a hospital experience. Almost automatically this isolation gave death a new and unfortunate aura. Death was hidden. It had to happen in the company of experts. It could not be dealt with in its natural setting, among the family in the community. The family came to feel useless. It induced horror or distaste. The children particularly came to think 'If it's so bad that they won't even let us be part of it, it must be awful'" (Hatfield & McHutchion, 1993, p. 30). When I think of my own experience with my grandmother's death, this last sentence resonates clearly. As a child, I was not even allowed to enter the building, much less the room where death was unfolding. They also refer to the family's feeling of being useless or helpless during the dying process, a notion discussed in the previous chapter.

Health professionals are socialized into a world where the sanctity of life holds a special place. Most of their education, training, and research is focussed on extending life. As Hansot (1996) states, "Physicians are trained to save lives, and most of us would not have it otherwise" (p. 151). However, when the doctors gave information to Hansot about her mother's condition and the likelihood of her recovery, their stories about the success of others in a similar condition "turned into so many cautionary tales. Most of the stories seemed to define success as survival and ended with the patient's departure from hospital. The quality of life after that departure was, at best, moot" (Hansot, 1996, p. 151). It would seem that in some circumstances health professionals have difficulty differentiating between living and merely surviving. Is there a way to balance health professionals' education, practice, and research so that both life and death can be valued and neither declared the enemy?

The media's role in disappearing death is rather paradoxical. A number of years ago, Kavanagh (1972) described his evening television viewing experience over a two-week period as follows: "I counted an average of 34 deaths at close range, countless more at a distance. Not one death raised as much as a slight tremor in me. Television feeds our fantasy of forever being a spectator. Even a bloody nose or a fainting spell by a fellow viewer would have aroused more emotion in me than a hundred deaths on the tube" (p. 13). I suspect that the death count on prime time television would be even higher today. Recent popular television series like *Law and Order*, *ER*, and *CSI: Crime Scene Investigation* revolve around stories of illness, injury, and death. In several of these dramas, the person—the victim—almost disappears as the focus shifts to solving the crime, attending to all the minutiae required to complete the puzzle and determine the cause or perpetrator of death. A sense that the case under investigation involved a person with a life, with relationships to others, with a future, is often lost. Is it possible that television and film have diminished our ability to distinguish between what is real and what is fantasy?

Satellite technology has made it possible to beam transmissions of death as they happen to our evening newscasts. During a recent newscast, a reporter warned viewers that what they were about to see was graphic. He then proceeded to show a young boy being shot to death as his father tried to shield him from the crossfire during an armed conflict in the city that was his home. I remember saying, under my breath, "Don't show the footage." I turned my head, not wanting to see what was happening, not wanting to believe it could be true, but I could not look away entirely. In this instance, I was able to discern that this depiction was authentic, but I wonder if children are able to make that distinction. Although death has not disappeared on television, I think the way in which it has been depicted has somehow desensitized us to it. I wonder if we now believe that everything we see on television or at the movies is illusion. What impact has this had on the way we think and act around death?

The language we use to describe death also contributes to its disappearance. In our conversations, the participants and I used euphemisms as a way to distance ourselves from death. We used phrases like "take me home," "go to her rest," "people's form of passing," "ready to go," "pull the plug," "pass away," "the end." Perhaps the most poetic was offered by a participant who used the phrase "waiting for the curtain to fall." One participant described how she found out that her husband was not to be resuscitated. She said, "I had just stepped out of the room when the intern came in and I watched through the crack in the door and they said to my husband, if you have a stroke, we're not going to try and save you and he [her husband] just nodded and smiled, nodded and smiled. He was ready to go." Although the word "death" is not present in the telling of this story, it is clearly at its heart.

living life

I consider myself a lucky person. I had a strong marriage (even though I never learned to sleep through Stuart's snoring; now I miss it). I've got wonderful kids and grandchildren. I've been healthy most of my life. I've had only one close call. When I was in my late fifties I was in a serious car accident (a friend of mine was driving) and had to undergo some complicated surgery. For a few days, it was touch and go whether I'd survive. But I was—I am—a fighter. As long as I was conscious, I wasn't going to give up. I was determined to get better. The power of the mind is amazing, absolutely amazing. If I hadn't had the will to live, I think I may have died. My recovery (after several months of physiotherapy and recuperation) was pretty much complete, and I was able to resume all of my previous activities. If I had been older, say in my eighties, I'm not sure I would have had the same will to go on. Even now I don't think I would want to go through what I did then. I've lived a good life. I've had many happy, fulfilling years, and if something awful were to happen and I wouldn't be able to return to my active lifestyle, I'd be much quicker to say, "Enough! Let me go!" I have no desire to live to be 100; I'd be bored! My life has always been worth living. So when it's time, it's going to be worth dying.

When I encounter the word "worth," I often think it is inter-changeable with the notion of value. When Alice says, "It's going to be worth dying," I interpret that to mean that there is some inherent value in dying. Kavanagh (1972) expresses a similar idea when he says, "Dying well is worth it, because it will insure I lived well, too. I am convinced that our personal failures to unearth, face, understand and accept our true feelings about death keep us from joyful living and dying as we choose. Our failures likewise keep us from treating those we love who are dying with the dignity they deserve" (p. 19).

One of the study participants differentiated between getting by in life and living more thoughtfully. He said, "Most people are living lives of quiet desperation. It's almost like a grave except it's open at both ends; it's just like a tunnel. They're locked in with mortgages, or marriages, or family matters they can't get out of or jobs they've got around their head because they've got to pay mortgages or kid's university fees. They're not happy but they can't make a change and they're totally frustrated, and so many people I talk to, if they'll admit, are like that. Most men don't admit it to other men. Women I think talk more about this but men don't. But if you really get them in a corner, they're not happy about life. So that's where I strongly feel that a person has to think of that third aspect. We are physical beings, we look after our physical needs and we workout and all this sort of thing. And mentally we train ourselves, we go to university and whatnot, but we have that spiritual side of us and if we don't do anything with that and haven't looked into that, then we're a very lean example of what a human being can be."

In reflecting upon her past history of cancer and coming to face her own mortality, one participant remarked, "Maybe it's supposed to be teaching me things, and I think in this time I think I've learned a lot about myself and about other people and life and all the rest of it." Difficult as it might be, reflecting upon one's mortality was perceived as beneficial by a number of study participants. How can this reflection be nurtured? Must one have had a difficult life experience like being diagnosed with cancer or losing a loved one before she is ready to think about her own mortality?

Brookes (1997) suggests, "Accepting finality can bring not only such quiet hopes but, in an unexpected way, a kind of truth, of freedom. Life, in fact" (p. 33). Similarly, L'Engle (1980), through the words of a dying grandfather, says, "If we knew each morning that there was going to be another morning, and on and on and on, we'd tend not to notice the sunrise, or hear the birds, or the waves rolling into shore. We'd tend not to treasure our time with the people we love. Simply the awareness that our mortal lives had a beginning and will have an end enhances the quality of our living" (p. 59). Scott-Maxwell (1968) suggests, "If we have hardly lived at all, it may be much harder to die" (p. 97). And yet another, a man who was dying from amyotrophic lateral sclerosis, shared the following insight: "Once you learn how to die, you learn how to live" (Albom, 1997, p. 82). These are strong claims. In essence, they suggest that one can only truly live life to its fullest after one has accepted death, particularly one's own death, as inevitable. The observation in my study that completing an advance directive gave individuals the opportunity to contemplate their own death suggests an added and crucial benefit that has received little attention in the literature. Is it possible that completing a living will might actually help one to live well? Such an outcome is difficult to measure in terms of a traditional cost/benefit analysis but seems worthy of further exploration. How do we learn to die? How do we learn to live?

In reflecting upon her life, Alice says it has been fulfilling and that she has been lucky. How did she reach this conclusion? Did she complete her own life review while preparing her advance directive? Must I do the same? If Alice were to say, "My life has been awful," would this impact her ability to complete an advance directive? Maybe I am not ready to assess my own life thoroughly. Have I achieved the goals I set for myself? (Some, but not all.) Have I treated people the way I should have? (Not always.) Have I made mistakes? (Definitely.) Maybe I need to re-evaluate my own life goals before I can define how I want my death to occur. Maybe I need to do more living before I can contemplate my own dying. Maybe it is easier if one is older or has been diagnosed with a serious illness to prepare a directive. Maybe one must be nearer to death, to be dying, before one can write a truly meaningful directive.

sitting quietly

For me, facing my own mortality seems a natural thing to do. Maybe it's because of the life experiences I've had; I'm not sure. But I do have friends who I think are hiding their heads in the sand. They just don't seem to be able to accept that death, their death, is a certainty. Maybe they're scared. I just don't see the point of getting all uptight about it. Death happens. I suppose if you don't believe in eternity, thinking about death would be more difficult. Maybe if you've never seen someone die, it's more frightening—fear of the unknown is powerful. Do I think there are advantages to accepting my own mortality? Definitely. It makes me appreciate every day that I have here on earth with my friends and family. I take time to sit quietly, to think, to reflect.

"In modern society, opportunities are rare for individuals to evaluate their life values and goals, change jobs or careers or emphasize different values" (Burgess, 1993, p. 46). In preparing their advance directives, most participants in my study took time to examine their lives and discuss their values and goals with their partners, their children, their friends. One participant stated, "I find with today's society, with all this rush and tear and television and the radio and everything we've got, that most people don't have hardly a moment of silence or introspection or time to read or anything, and that's pretty sad. And it sometimes takes funerals or accidents to bring them up short and that's too bad because their life might have been quite different had they had more time or made time to stop and think, and I think a personal directive can do that." Higgins (1993) writes, "Most of us have lived unreflective lives, preoccupied with living, and rarely have thought about the core issues of life and death, and definitely not about our own eventual death. Often, only suffering forces us to face the mystery of being, to ask the age-old existential questions, 'Who am I? Where did I come from? Where do I go?'" (p. 55). In a fictional account of an elderly woman's death, the character Sarton (1973) has created says, "I see, now that death is not a vague prospect but something I hold in my hand, that the very opposite is required from what I thought at first. I am asked to listen to music, look at the bare trees divested of all but their fine structure, drink in the sunset like wine, read poetry again" (pp. 125–126). How can we learn to sit quietly, to contemplate life and death, amidst the backdrop of our busy lives? If we are to truly appreciate life, it seems that we must turn our attention to facing our own mortality.

talking
ABOUT DEATH

3

*For me, my mother had always been there, and I
had never seriously thought that some day, that
soon I should see her go. Her death, like her birth,
had its place in some legendary time. When I said
to myself "She is of an age to die" the words were
devoid of meaning, as so many words are.*

(de Beauvoir, 1965, p. 20)

conversing at the dinner table

*I don't remember the first conversation I had about death with my own chil-
dren, but death was never swept under the rug in our home. My children's
first encounter with the permanence of death was when one of their pets
died. Over the years, we had an assortment of birds, fish, cats, and dogs, and
even an injured rabbit rescued from the wild. When a pet died, it received a
burial in the backyard with everyone recounting a favourite memory of time
spent with it. Dusk seemed to be the appointed time for these ceremonies.*

*I can recall, too, many lively conversations at the dinner table where
we debated the pros and cons of issues like euthanasia, organ donation, and
suicide. It sounds kind of morbid, but we even joked about the clothes my
husband and I would be buried in. When my husband died, my son found
it odd that we had to make a decision about what kind of suit to put on
his dad, especially considering he was being cremated. So we got chatting
about it and my son said, "Don't worry about it, Mom. I know exactly what
we're going to do for you." And I said with some trepidation, "Really,
what are you going to do?" He said, "We're going to dress you up in your
favourite caftan." (I happen to love wearing caftans; they're tremendously
comfortable for lounging about! I'm not sure I would have ever thought of
being cremated in one, but it wasn't a half-bad idea.) He continued, "And at
your church service, we'll put your wooden spoon in the foyer. That will be a
symbol of you as a teacher and a mother." You see, I used the wooden spoon
as a motivational tool when I taught, and I'm also a pretty good cook.*

*We've always been able to talk and joke about these sorts of things
openly in our family, so it seemed only natural that I would include my
children fully in the process of preparing my advance directive.*

For participants in the study I conducted, preparing an advance directive often seemed to provide an opening for a candid discussion about their death and dying. In conversations between parents and their children about the parent's future death and dying, it was sometimes the older adult who broached the topic with a child; less often it was the child who arrived laden with information on advance directives. These discussions unfolded in a variety of ways—an informal chat at the kitchen table with one child, a formal family meeting with all of the children and their spouses in attendance, a series of conversations that spanned months or years. Sometimes the discussions were difficult, uncomfortable; other times they were gentle, unrestrained. For those in this study who were married, the preparation of an advance directive was a joint project completed by both husband and wife. All had engaged in deep discussions with their spouse, and they shared the decision-making process. There was not always immediate agreement, but satisfactory resolution was achieved in the end.

During these discussions, spouses and children indicated that they learned things about the other that they had not previously known. In talking about conversations she had with her son about her advance directive, one participant said, "What you really want is not always discussed as much as it should be. This [our talking about my directive] has made, I believe, my son and I get much closer and he will say sometimes when we are talking, 'I didn't know that, Mom. I didn't know you wanted that.' So good, I'm glad we brought it up."

Similarly, one of the married participants recounted, "We had a lot of talk with each other as to what I should put in mine and what my wife should put in hers and why we were doing what we were doing, if it was any different...There were differences in the sense that I was quite readily able to say who I wanted to be my agent and so on. When my wife got going on hers, I noticed I wasn't in the same position as she was in my will, and I asked why. She said, 'Well, when it comes to a woman, I think there's certain situations where a man wouldn't feel comfortable; therefore, I want my daughter to take control in those areas.' I firmly feel that the less the better, the less attempts at heroics, if there's any. If there's no question that the pathway is downhill fast or even if it's straight along for years, if it's in a comatose state, there's no reason I want to be a burden on the system or the family.

So, I'll make sure they understand that and I think they know that's what I'd like and my wife was the same. And she's 10 years younger. I was amazed. She too figures that she's lived a very excellent life to this point and if she has to go, well that's fine, don't go on." What is suggested through these excerpts and is borne out in the research literature (for example, Coppola, Ditto, Danks, & Smucker, 2001; Sansone & Phillips, 1995; Sonneblick, Friedlander, & Steinberg, 1993) is that family members may not be able to predict accurately the preferences of their loved ones for life-sustaining treatment without having focussed and ongoing conversations about end-of-life issues.

The story of Alice's caftan and the wooden spoon stimulates many questions for me about symbols. What is a symbol? Why are they important? The definition of symbol applicable to this discussion is something that "stands for, represents, or denotes something else" (Oxford English Dictionary, 2002). Chisholm (as cited in Oxford English Dictionary, 2002) is attributed as saying in 1946 that "our distinguishing human characteristic is that we are symbol-users." How would I want my life to be symbolized? How would I want my death to be marked? In describing what they valued in life, what was important to them, or how they wanted to be remembered, participants used phrases such as, "I try to live each day without regret," "I want to be remembered as a person that had a real spark of life," and "independence, pride, and dignity." One of the participants talked about the discussion he had with his granddaughters, who were to inherit his coin collection. He told them, "If you have to sell them, that will be your decision, but remember your granddad loved these coins." For this participant, his coin collection represented something symbolic, beyond its monetary value. In Alice's story about symbols, there is levity and humour, but when I try to answer questions about my life, tears well up in my eyes. I am evidently not ready yet to contemplate these questions. How can I become better prepared and able to respond to these queries, to assimilate the inevitability of my death into my own set of beliefs and practices?

Remen (1996), the author of a book entitled *Kitchen Table Wisdom*, talks about the significance of the kitchen table to our understanding of life. She says, "Everybody is a story. When I was a child, people sat around kitchen tables and told their stories. We don't do that so much anymore. Sitting around the table telling stories is not just a way of passing time. It is the way the wisdom gets passed along. The stuff that helps us to live a life worth remembering. Despite the awesome powers of technology many of us still do not live very well. We may need to listen to each other's stories once again" (p. xxvii). Participants in my study talked about discussing death around the kitchen table. One participant recalled, "Most of the time, like during supper hour, we would discuss certain things and/or I would mention it [whatever was on the news—euthanasia, organ donation, etc.] to one of the children as we think about it and when it came to the supper table, we would open it up. You know, one of us would open it up or usually I was the one that would bring up the subject." Perhaps it was not coincidental that all but 1 of the 15 conversations I had with participants transpired around dining tables. It seemed to be a comfortable place where individuals were willing to talk and a cup of tea could be enjoyed. I think Remen is correct when she suggests that families do not sit down together for supper as often as they once did. The opportunities for sharing stories with one another are more limited. How can people be encouraged to gather at the kitchen table once again? What can be done to ensure that the wisdom of one generation is passed on to the next?

joking about death

I'm not sure why my children and I are able to talk about death so openly. That certainly wasn't the case in my own youth. Although my mother died at home, I don't remember ever having a conversation about her death with my father. It happened. It was finished. End of story. I do recall trying to mention it to him on a couple of occasions. Tears would well up in his eyes, and he'd turn and walk away. I soon quit trying, because it hurt me to see my father cry. Christine, my youngest, is a little like that. She's the one who tears up during sentimental TV commercials. But we seem to be able to joke about death. Tearfulness doesn't stop us from talking.

Humour was a strategy that many participants used both in the context of our conversations about preparing an advance directive and in the discussions they had with their own families and friends. One participant convened a family meeting of sorts to discuss both the contents of her advance directive and her estate will. As she continued, some of her children began chuckling. Before going any further, she asked them what they were laughing about. The story unfolds as follows: "My son said, 'We know this is serious. But we're just using a comic gesture here and there just to break the would-be tension. So that there isn't any tension, we're wisecracking, but we're taking it all in.' I said, 'Well, I'm glad to know that because, (laughs) I mean, if I thought that you were really not interested or something,' I said, 'I really would be concerned.' And they assured me that, 'No, no, they realized that this was something that I was very serious about'... They questioned here and there, and apparently the answers, some of the answers, must have suited them (laughs). So I felt very good after having them all here and having the discussion." This participant's demeanour was exuberant and she laughed often during our conversation. From the description she provided of her meeting with her children, it seems that they have inherited a similar jovial nature.

Another participant described a conversation she had with her son about her obituary. "I've said this, you know, in joking, for example, when you put in my obit [obituary], don't you dare put in a picture of when I was 20 because I've earned this face, you know. And my son just kind of chuckled and he says, 'I know which picture you're getting and it's none of your business.' You know, but I mean, he knows, you know, this is teasing." Similarly, another participant said, "I tease my daughters that I have to be nice to them because they get to choose where I live if I become unable to look after myself."

One of the participants, who had not yet talked with his children about his directive, had some specific wishes about his future. (For instance, he wanted classical music played in his room.) In anticipating the discussion with his children he said, "They'll get a laugh when we talk about those things or why this is important to me." Another participant suggested that certain cultures approach death with more humour. She said, "There's certainly, in our culture, lots of very humorous stories and songs and writings about people's form of passing...There's 'Finigan's Wake.' It's an Irish one [song] that's very funny about the way that Finigan passed on, only he didn't!" Finigan was an Irish man who enjoyed his liquor. After falling from a ladder, his family and friends thought he was dead. At his wake, when a gallon of whiskey is accidentally spilled upon him, he is revived and surprises everyone in attendance (Glover, 1864).

Humour is that quality of action, speech, or writing which excites amusement; oddity, jocularity, facetiousness, comicality, and fun (Oxford English Dictionary, 2002). Humour is considered to have a sympathetic quality that is allied to pathos (Oxford English Dictionary, 2002). Historically, the word "humour" described the four primary fluids of the body (blood, phlegm, choler, and melancholy), which were responsible for controlling one's physical and mental health (Oxford English Dictionary, 2002). If humour was used by participants as a coping strategy, as a way of dealing with difficult subject matter, the link between the historical usage of the word and its current application becomes more visible. Participants seem to be using humour to help maintain their own physical and psychological well being. I had not considered before a connection between humour and pathos, that humour might be something through which a person makes connections and shares emotions with another. I have, however, often thought that people without a sense of humour must be lonely, and this interpretation seems to support that conjecture. Laughing alone simply does not compare to laughing with another person. What does this mean for the many isolated seniors who are living alone without family members or friends nearby? How can one's sense of humour be nourished? Can people learn to incorporate humour into their daily life, particularly as they face difficult end-of-life issues?

widening the discussion

After the seminar that Susan and I attended, we talked a bit about the kind of things I was thinking of including in my directive. Over the next few months, I had the opportunity to chat informally with each of my children, keeping them informed as I proceeded to complete my directive. I bounced ideas off them. I asked them to read what I had written. I asked if they understood what I was saying, and if there were other things they would like to see included. When it was finished (as finished as it can be for the time being at least), I invited them all over, along with their spouses, one Sunday afternoon so that we could go over it in some detail. I wanted them all in attendance so that any points of disagreement could be resolved.

There were moments of awkwardness, of nervous laughter, especially when we began the discussion, but they quickly dissipated. Dealing with *their father's illness and the way his death unfolded was a traumatic experience for us all, so my motivation in completing the document was clear to them. They were all very supportive. I have fond memories of that afternoon. In that moment, I felt close to my children, and I think they felt the same way. Because we are all so busy, these kinds of opportunities don't happen as often as they should. Scheduling the time to have the discussion was important for us all. I think involving my family in the process of preparing my advance directive has made us a stronger unit than ever before.*

Many participants in the study I conducted recognized the importance of sharing the process of end-of-life decision-making with family members and friends, especially the ones who were stakeholders who would be directly affected by the decisions made. One participant had not yet undertaken the step of reviewing his directive with his children, but planned to do so in the near future. When I met with him, both he and his wife were putting the final touches on their documents. He said, "We haven't met with them [our children] yet, but we will be sitting down with them as a family. And with our family that's easy to do, an evening at home and just discuss it. If you don't do that with a regular will, too, you end up with all kinds of hard feelings later that are unjustified, but if they know your feelings and why you've said what you've said, it should clear up a lot of that. And the same thing with the unwritten part of the directive, the side documents that go only to your agent. I'll make sure that they know there is this side document and what it says and why I've done it that way." This individual had been counselled to prepare two documents. One is for public consumption and outlines only his basic wishes; the other is for his agents only and provides greater details. His purpose in constructing his directive this way is to provide his agents with greater latitude in the decision-making process. The side documents, as he called them, are intended to be used as guidelines by his agents, rather than interpreted literally as fact.

Kuczewski (1996) suggests that family members should be part of the medical decision-making process, and he prescribes a certain role for them. He believes that family members, through the simple practice of sharing life stories and experiences, can help individuals to identify and articulate the values that are most important to them and to the decision at hand. Those family members engaged in the story-telling process, he indicates, may also undergo their own journey of self-discovery. It is through our relationships with each other (family, friend, or stranger), and by sharing stories about life with one another, that we learn more about the individual and about ourselves. As I participated in conversations with older adults in my study, I continuously reflected upon my own values, my own life. As I tried to come to an understanding of their experience, I also sought an understanding of my self and the meaning of my life.

Healthcare providers to date have focussed their attention almost exclusively on the physical body—on symptoms and physiological outcomes—and have largely failed to acknowledge how health and well-being are affected by the subjective experiences of the individual, by his or her life story. Perrin (1997) affirms, "A medical directive is of little use if the individual has merely completed the form without engaging in a discussion of his/her desires with family and physician. It is the discussion of the patient's goals, values, and desires during the preparation of the directive that allows the family and healthcare provider to ascertain what the patient would have wished if the actual situation does not exactly match the anticipated scenario. When medical directives were initially proposed, it was assumed that such discussion would necessarily result" (p. 22). Why has this not routinely happened? Why are healthcare professionals so infrequently involved in the process of preparing a directive with their patients? Perhaps we need to do more to encourage healthcare professionals to elicit and listen to the stories of patients.

One participant had a family friend who was a nurse with a special interest in counselling persons in the preparation of advance directives. The two spent several afternoons discussing various end-of-life issues together. As she says, "It's very difficult for me to remain business-like when she's here because she is like a daughter and we have such good fun together and I've felt bad after she's left that I've, you know, wasted her time. But she enjoys coming, too, I know. I find that she is very precise and has done excellent work with the right questions and the explanations and, you know, if she is as kind and objective to everybody as she is to me, this is fantastic, she's at the right place." Many of the participants in my study were in positions where they had access to resources, both human and educational, to assist them in the process of preparing an advance directive. How can health professionals ensure equitable access to such resources for all? Do health professionals need to be more engaged in providing education and counselling around end-of-life decision-making? Are there ways in which wider discussion of the issues can be promoted? How can health professionals ensure that everyone has someone they can talk to about death?

considering a parent's death

If you were to ask me whether talking about my death with my children was easy, I would probably have to say no. It wasn't easy, but it wasn't difficult either. I don't think any child, small or grown up, likes to think about the death of his or her parent. A conversation I had a while back with my son is a perfect example. One afternoon David brought me a delightful little book called The Love of Mothers and Sons, *and I asked him to write a message on the inside cover. We had been discussing my directive earlier that day, so he wrote something about our good relationship and finished with, "And will you please stop talking about your death!" We both laughed. That's the kind of lightness we were able to tackle preparing a directive with, and I'm very pleased about that.*

One of my neighbours, Mary, has had a much more difficult time talking about death with her two sons. Mary has had some serious health problems in recent years and feels that her death is a distinct possibility within the not too distant future. She wants her sons to be prepared, but she has been met with resistance. Mary says her boys will not talk about her death or her wish to be cremated. She worries they will think their father is being cheap if he doesn't spend money on a fancy casket for her, even though she has told them her wish many times. They also will not discuss dividing her possessions. She has asked each son, Steven and Michael, separately on several occasions if there is something in particular in the house that they would like to have. They always say, "No, Mom, we don't need anything." Finally, after multiple attempts, she wore Steven down, and he said there is one thing he really likes—the sculpture of the dolphins. Armed with the ammunition that Steven had made a decision, she once more asked the same question of Michael. He said, "I don't want to talk about it, but if there was one thing, it would be the dolphins." Poor Mary!

Not long ago, Mary told me another kind of funny but sad story that took place when Michael came to visit. The two of them were in the basement sorting some things and Mary said, "When I'm gone I want you to get rid of all the junk in the basement." Michael turned to her and said, "But where are you going, Ma?" Michael just wasn't getting it. He wasn't ready to accept the fact that his mother will die one day. Mary has pretty much given up for now and doesn't even bother bringing up the subject. Her husband hasn't been much help, because things like this were never talked about in his family. He'll tolerate a discussion, but he's not keen to talk about death either.

For now, Mary has stopped bringing up the subject of her own death. To ensure that her sons will have the necessary information and be able to understand the decisions her husband might make on her behalf, should she die before him, she has written her wishes in an advance directive and an estate will. One is left wondering, though, why Steven and Michael are having such a difficult time talking about their mother's inevitable, although not necessarily imminent, death. Michael's comment, "But where are you going, Ma?," is almost humorous, as if he thinks his mother is talking about moving to the house down the street. He does not acknowledge that "going" is a euphemism for "dying." It would appear that each son has come up with a response to the question: "Is there anything in the house you would like?" in order to pacify their mother and to bring to a close any conversation about her death.

One wonders how a generational pattern of not talking about death can be broken. Mary has attempted to change this pattern in her family, but has been largely unsuccessful. On the other hand, Alice has met with greater success. One wonders how the experience of death and dying is transformed by these discussions. If Mary had been able to enter into a more thoughtful discussion about death and dying with her sons, would this change how her own death and dying would unfold? In considering a parent's death, it is almost impossible not to consider one's own mortality. Is the stumbling block that Mary's sons are not yet ready to confront their own mortality? What will need to happen in order for Mary to have greater success in talking to her sons in the future? How can she help her sons face her own and their own mortality?

Although there has been considerable study of the adult child's reaction to a parent's death, I located only a few studies that focus on the adult child's anticipation of a parent's death. Kowalski (1986) suggests that when anticipating their parent's death, adult children may fear becoming orphans, worry that certain issues with their parents will not be resolved, and be compelled to face their own mortality. Fitzgerald (1994), in a grounded theory study with six adult children who had or were anticipating the loss of their parents, identifies three major processes for adult children who are facing the loss of their parents: 1) asking questions about life and death, 2) evaluating relationships with parents, and 3) preparing themselves to outlive their parents.

In my study, several participants described situations that reflect these fears and processes. One participant believed that the discussions about her death were helping her son to "think of his ends." Alternatively, another participant said, "They [my children] don't want to look at it [death]. When you prepare a will, you're preparing for your death...that it exists, that's right. And I know my children have that attitude sometimes...I think it's a thing that says, you know, Mom and Dad are getting old and who would like to think that Mom and Dad are getting old." This participant continued to be optimistic that with enough repetition and positive reinforcement, his children will become more accepting of their own and their parents' inevitable death.

In anticipation of her husband's death from cancer, another participant and her husband both wrote advance directives. She describes her son's reactions to his father's anticipated death this way. "We knew he was leaving. He knew he was leaving. We could connect, we could talk about things. Like my son said, he felt very guilty being away for the six years, but as time went on, and the more and more that he had to do things for his dad...then he started to relax, he didn't feel guilty." Another participant said, "We did have a lot of discussion, not only on the physical, but on the psychological, the emotional level for myself and for the children." According to Kavanagh (1972), "Helping children gain an ease around death prevents the many fearful approaches to life we see in ourselves and in those around us. The main purpose in openly discussing death with children is to enable them to live more freely...The wonder and glory of life is the gist of our message not the morbidity of death" (pp. 131–132).

In describing the older adult's experience of talking about death with their children in the context of preparing a directive, there

were three approaches that seemed most evident—avoidance, acquiescence, and acceptance. Avoidance represents a desire not to talk
about a parent's death. Acquiescence suggests that a parent's death
is acknowledged, that no objection is raised, and that the conversation is tolerated but limited. Acceptance suggests that the children
welcomed and regarded the discussion as favourable. These categories
are neither exhaustive nor mutually exclusive. Rather, they represent
three sub-themes that appeared in the data. Across all three—avoidance, acquiescence, and acceptance—there is a sense that facing a
parent's death is not easy or natural—that it is a significant event for
all involved, perhaps even especially for adult children. Kavanagh
(1972), in his book entitled *Facing Death*, describes one adult child's
experience this way: "A handsome corpsman in the navy, intense and
terror-eyed, Van told of his perennial need to anticipate his parents'
death. He was obsessed with their imagined death and his equally
imagined grief. Nightly, he pictured them in caskets, waked and buried them, unable to sleep until he pre-felt his untested grief" (p. 89).

Clearly for some, anticipating a parent's death is a difficult and disturbing process. Although the children were not interviewed in the
study I conducted, we see glimpses of these difficulties in Michael's
comment "Where are you going, Ma?" and in David's admonition
"Will you please stop talking about your death!" Another participant
who raised the topic with her daughter said, "When I first mentioned
the directive to her she got all teary-eyed and said, 'Oh, Mom,' and
I just said, 'Hey it's a fact of life, you live, you die, and I have to do
this.'" I can empathize with these comments because I find it hard
to imagine a world without my parents. In the opening quotation of
this chapter, de Beauvoir (1965) eloquently captures the difficulty that
children of all ages have in imagining a parent's death in this phrase
about her mother: "Her death...had its place in some legendary time"
(p. 20). How can adult children come to accept that the "legendary
time" may be now?

imposing limits on the discussion

*While I prepared my own directive, I talked to several friends about the
process. It's interesting how we have all approached it somewhat differently. One friend, Isobel, has had two bouts of breast cancer. She has
completed an advance directive and shared its contents with her four*

*children, but she did not include them much in the process. Instead she
talked with a close friend who is a nurse and a breast cancer survivor.
Isobel believes her friend is in a better position to understand how she is
thinking and feeling than her children. Isobel believes she is protecting her
children by limiting the discussion about her death with them, but I'm not
so sure. Sometimes I wonder if she is shutting them out. I think there are
real benefits to having open discussions with your children. For me, I think
it has brought our family closer together. Everyone feels that they have an
important role to play, that they can help, that they can say what's on their
mind and be heard.*

Isobel's rationale for leaving her children out of the decision-
making process is to protect them, but one wonders whether this
action will achieve the results she hopes for or rather create distance
between mother and children. In this situation, it would seem that
Isobel is almost forcing her children to avoid entering into a discussion about her end-of-life. In an effort to protect them from hurt and
harm, is she actually preventing them from engaging deeply with her
about her death and dying? Who will be at Isobel's bedside when she
is dying? How will her children feel when someone else is making
decisions about their mother? With one of the study participants, it
was the children who set a limit to the discussion around death. In
this instance the discussion was centred on the participant's estate
will. He said, "When we had our wills made and we gave them a copy
of our will, we said, 'This is the will.' And my daughter said, 'I'm not
even going to open this, I don't want to look at it. I'm going to put it
away, I know it's there.' And I told her, she's the executor. And she
said, 'I don't want to look at it; I don't even want to think about it,
okay?'" So the participant said okay, and the matter was closed. From
what other participants shared, and what is written in the literature,
it seems important that the communication channels remain open.
How can we, all of us, keep the conversation going?

talking to no one

*A friend of my husband, John, left home when he was very young and has
been on his own ever since. He never married and for as long as we have
known him, he has been estranged from most of his family. He is a private
man and didn't really talk with anyone before or while he was preparing*

his directive. In fact, the only reason I know that he has a directive is that it came up in conversation when he was over for dinner one night. I mentioned that I was preparing my directive, and he said that he had signed one too. From the little that he said about it, I got the sense that under no circumstances did he want his life to be prolonged in any way. He had lived his life independently, and it seemed that he wanted to die that way too. It seemed sad to me that he had no one to share these sorts of decisions with. He had lived all of his adult life alone, and I was now picturing him dying alone. I guess it fits with his lifestyle. I guess it is the right thing for him. Yet I feel concern that there is no one he can count on to speak up on his behalf.

For those participants who didn't have a spouse or children, it was a niece or nephew, a sibling, or a trusted friend that was usually involved in discussions about preparing an advance directive. Some participants chose individuals they thought would have an understanding of the purpose of advance directives and have some knowledge of death and dying, such as a nurse or a lawyer. One participant shared, "We talk, you know—about things so that she knows. And we will continue to talk. Well, I think because she's a nurse I thought that she would be, you know, in a good position to [understand]...And also we're probably closer than I am to some of my other nieces and nephews because she lived here for six years and we spent, you know, quite a bit of time together at that time and so, you know, she's probably the closest to me." They selected individuals whom they believed would accept this role willingly. Only one older man completed his directive as a solitary act. His only communication with others about his wishes was to provide a copy of his directive to his family doctor. After meeting with him, I wondered if his decision to participate in my study fulfilled an unmet need or desire to talk about what he had done, about his own death, with another.

When I began the process of completing my own advance directive, I, too, approached it as a solitary act. I gathered a variety of templates, was very familiar with the legislation, and thought I had everything necessary to complete the project in hand. That is my usual approach to performing tasks: collect what you need and just do it. I think I am a capable, self-directed person. I do not like to be dependent upon others. However, as I sat in front of the computer, staring at the blank screen, I was immobilized. I look out the window. The sun has started to burn through the heavy fog silently hanging in the cold winter air. Clear blue sky is slowly unfolding. The branches on the trees are still. Every few seconds a car passes by, and I hear the muted sound of its engine. Maybe it is too quiet here in my livingroom. I get up from the chair and turn the radio on, just loud enough to provide some background noise. Now that I am up, I refill my water glass and get a snack from the kitchen. Almost an hour has gone by since I began this task. Progress has been painstakingly slow. Is it possible that completing an advance directive requires the input of others, that it is not easily done alone and in isolation, that talking about death is an essential aspect of the process? If so, what happens to those who have no one with whom to dialogue about death? How can we, as healthcare providers and healthcare recipients, begin to widen the discussion? How can we learn to talk more openly about death? How can we ensure that everyone has the opportunity to talk about death?

choosing
AN ALLY

4

"Don't leave me in the power of the brutes."
I thought of all those who have no one to
make that appeal to: what agony it must be
to feel oneself a defenceless thing, utterly at
the mercy of indifferent doctors and over-
worked nurses. No hand on the forehead
when terror seizes them; no sedative as soon
as pain begins to tear them; no lying prattle
to fill the silence of the void.

(de Beauvoir, 1965, p. 94)

naming an agent

In Alberta's legislation, individuals can name in their directive, one or more person(s)—referred to as an agent—to make decisions for them should there come a time when they are no longer able to make decisions for themselves (like if the individual is unconscious or has Alzheimer's disease). Naming an agent seemed a sensible thing for me to do, because no matter how many specific instructions I include in my written directive, there may be a situation that I haven't thought about, or the circumstances might be different from what I had envisioned. With advances in technology happening so quickly, you never know what tomorrow will bring, let alone five years down the road. So, you want your agent to have some flexibility to interpret what you have written. I've given mine carte blanche in any decision they make as long as they think it is in my best interest at the time. I've even given them the power to make decisions about determining my mental capacity. I may be going out on a limb with that one, but I figure they know my usual state of mind better than any physician. So, in consultation with a physician, they can decide whether or not I am acting as my usual self, or if my mind is slipping and I am behaving out of character.

Naming an agent was perceived by participants as both a backup and an adjunct to preparing an advance directive. As a backup, participants believed their agents would act in such a way as to reinforce and uphold the written statements they had made. As an adjunct, participants believed their agents could provide supplemental information that would contextualize their written statements. In both circumstances, the agent would be acting in support of the maker of the directive's goals, as an ally. As Alice clearly identifies, another reason for naming an agent is to deal with the issue of uncertainty. Illnesses that are today considered terminal and life-threatening may in a matter of years (and before Alice has a chance to update her advance directive accordingly) become treatable through the development of new medications, surgical procedures, and so forth. Alice has provided her agents with the freedom to make decisions that they think are best given the current set of circumstances and their knowledge of her values and approach to life and death. As one study participant reflected upon the role of an agent, he said, "He knows you well enough as to know what you would desire and then he can make the decision and you are literally giving him that flexibility and that power. If you're confident in who you appoint as agent, it shouldn't bother you." Another participant indicated, "You've got to choose a person who's going to be there. If you choose, in my opinion, an outside party, who do you choose? Who would you choose? You know, say we'll choose a good friend; friends come and go! They move away. You have to be sure that it's going to be somebody who's going to be available and there at all times."

Situations have been described in the literature and the popular press about advance directives that were either ignored by healthcare professionals or the treatment provided was inconsistent with written or verbal instructions (Edson, 1993; Hansot, 1996; Teno, Licks et al., 1997). In the widely published SUPPORT study undertaken in the United States, as few as 35 percent of physicians were aware that their seriously ill and hospitalized patients had prepared directives and that they were present in the patients' charts (Teno, Lynn et al., 1997). Clearly, there was a breakdown in communication and subsequent lack of knowledge about patients' wishes around life-sustaining treatment in these situations. In these circumstances, an agent might have played an important role in ensuring that the physicians providing care were aware of the documents and familiar with the nature of their contents.

Perhaps even more disturbing are those situations where healthcare providers knowingly provide treatment that is in opposition to the written wishes of an individual. The rationale for providing such treatment does not usually represent any malicious intent on the part of care providers. Sometimes health professionals initiate treatment because they believe that the individual will survive if they receive life-sustaining treatment, and that it is their duty to treat, to provide at the least an opportunity for continued life. Sometimes it is provided because the healthcare providers do not believe that the individual understood the potential consequences of what he or she had written. In both of these instances, an agent who has engaged in meaningful discussions with the maker of the directive may be in the best position to intervene and advocate on behalf of the patient.

Advocating on behalf of a patient may not be easy; indeed it may be very difficult. Elisabeth Hansot (1996), a 57-year-old professional woman who was her mother's agent describes her experience this way. "I am astounded that I had so little inkling of how hard it would be to help my mother have the death she wanted...When we talked together about how she wanted to die, she was clear, consistent, and matter-of-fact. She hoped for a swift death and wanted no unnecessary prolongation of her life...I believed that I could make decisions on her behalf as she would want them made if she were to become incapacitated. As it turned out, I was woefully unprepared for what was in store for her and for me" (p. 149). Hansot came up against the "power of the brutes" that de Beauvoir speaks of in this chapter's opening quotation. In the hospital setting, the physicians in charge of Hansot's mother carried the bulk of the power, and a five-day battle ensued. Her mother's physician, according to Hansot, "found it nearly impossible to accept that my mother would prefer death to living with hemiparalysis and a tracheotomy" (p. 149). De Beauvoir also speaks of the difficulty she had in ensuring her mother's wishes were enacted. "When I reached home, all the sadness and horror of these last days dropped upon me with all its weight. And I too had a cancer eating into me—remorse. 'Don't let them operate on her.' And I had not prevented anything" (p. 57). I wonder if the individuals who the study participants have selected as agents are prepared for combat. I also wonder if there is another way to approach these difficult end-of-life decisions without using a war metaphor—without defining the situation as "us against them," or life against death. Is there a way to reconceptualize the conflict, or even better, to prevent a conflict from emerging? Until such a shift in our stance occurs, choosing an ally will remain a crucial aspect of ensuring that one's wishes for end-of-life sustaining treatment will be respected.

The concept of power as it relates to end-of-life decision-making is important to consider further. Power, in this context, means the ability to do or to act (Barber, 2001). Within healthcare provider/patient relationships, historically, it has been the healthcare provider who holds the most power, by virtue of his or her knowledge and role as gatekeeper to healthcare resources. However, when end-of-life decisions are being made, one might rightfully ask, "Who ought to hold the power?" Many have concluded that patients ought to have more say in what happens to them at the end-of-life, and the trend toward legalization of advance directives is partly an effort to correct this existing power imbalance. In many jurisdictions, the notion of power is even captured in legal terminology (for example, Power of Attorney for Personal Care). The concept of power also fits within the war metaphor that permeates end-of-life literature. It is usually the most powerful who win wars. Healthcare providers need to be cognizant of the power imbalances that exist in their relationships with patients, and they must act to ensure that patients are empowered to make end-of-life decisions that reflect their wishes.

In the study I conducted, healthcare professionals were rarely named as agents. Several participants, however, indicated that assessment of competency could be undertaken in consultation with a physician. The determination of competency was one area where participants believed that healthcare professionals had special expertise. As the data analysis proceeded in my study, the lack of involvement of healthcare professionals crystallized in a number of ways—in initiating discussions, in participating in discussions, in the process of preparing directives, and in their enactment. There was a general perception among participants that healthcare professionals, physicians in particular, have different beliefs and goals from older adults about life-sustaining treatment. For this group of participants, quality of life was generally of greater significance and value than quantity of life. Several indicated they were concerned that physicians would provide treatment that was more aggressive than they desired. One of the participants thought there had been a shift in attitudes in recent years. He said, "There's more acceptance now, I think, in the younger medical doctors but at that time [in the 1980s], I think they thought, 'My job is to save lives. I don't care if he's a vegetable, he's alive.'" Although the participants recognize that this mindset is important in sustaining continued progress and advances in medicine, they did not want it to apply to them in end-of-life situations.

selecting the best agent

I remember the lawyer talking about some qualities he recommended in an agent. First of all, he suggested that you name someone who is going to be readily available when needed. Second, he said that you want someone who knows you well, who knows the things you value, and is knowledgeable about what's in your directive. And it has to be someone you trust, someone you know will respect your wishes, and someone who will be able to make the tough decisions if needed.

For me, the obvious choices were my children. I've put my son, David, first on the list. He'll be the primary contact for decisions about my care. David is level-headed, bright, able to face serious issues head on—he's an iron-solid person with no mental or emotional weaknesses that might jeopardize advocating the care I would want. I think having only one person identified as the key contact has the added benefit of improving communication between the healthcare providers and the family. The healthcare team will know whom they need to relay information to, which hopefully will streamline the process. I can imagine it must be frustrating and time-consuming for physicians and nurses to keep repeating information to one family member after another, and to have to answer the same questions over and over again. (I know it's tiring for me when I have to repeat myself.) This way, my son will be in the position to share the information with other family members, particularly my daughters, and to gather and consolidate all of their questions and concerns.

Susan and Christine will be my alternate agents in case David is unavailable, and they will be the ones in charge of decisions about where I should live, whom I should socialize with, and those sorts of things. These are areas where they feel more comfortable. They know the kinds of things I look for in a place to live (clean toilets and bathtubs, lots of windows, flowering plants). But I expect all decisions to be shared among the three of them. They seem okay with this idea. It is really important to me that they continue to be friends after I'm out of the picture. It is my hope that knowing what I want ahead of time and having these discussions will help to achieve that goal.

If an individual's autonomy is to be respected, it is vital for a substitute decision-maker to be knowledgeable about the patient's desires and willing to act accordingly (Sansone & Phillips, 1995; Yamani, Fleming, Brensilver, & Brandstetter, 1995). Although the adult children's perspectives were not directly accessed in the study I conducted, one gets a sense from participants that they believed their children were well equipped and prepared to assume this role. As Alice relates, David is "level-headed, bright, able to face serious issues head on." One study participant said, "I'm quite sure my kids will respect them [my wishes] and I don't know who else would be very much involved. I think they'll be right there if I'm very ill."

The tendency of older adults with children to name their children to be their agents (Sansone & Phillips, 1995) was reflected in this group of participants. There is some evidence to suggest that substitute decision-makers take their role seriously. In a survey by Sansone and Phillips (1995) on the topic of advance directives, 168 substitute decision-makers of older adults received a questionnaire by mail. Responses were received from 153 individuals, an incredibly high response rate, which suggests that the topic was one of significance to this group. Seventy percent of the respondents were adult children. In my study, the involvement of most of the adult children in formal and informal family discussions, and in posing mindful questions, suggests that this group of children also approached the role of substitute decision-maker with a high degree of thoughtfulness and sincerity.

In the following quotation, a study participant describes the many factors she contemplated when deciding on an agent. "I think I appointed my son because, in general, men are the ones who usually have the authority of making decisions and signing for this and that and the other, more so than women. And my second child is my daughter and she has cerebral palsy, and I don't think that she would want to have that responsibility put on her. And also he has a phone and answering machine, whereas she doesn't. Well, she does too, but she never listens to it, darn it! And you have to phone her at least three days in a row and she might get around to it the fourth day and figure, 'What did you call me the other day for?' 'Well, why didn't you phone me back the first day?' 'Well, I didn't find out!' So, I mean,

I definitely don't want her to be in charge! And the third child is the other daughter who is quite capable...[but she] has lived far away from home since she graduated from university and went up north to work. So, I mean, I would not name her because she is never in the city."

Another participant named both a primary and alternate agent. Projecting himself into a time of future incapacity he explained, "I thought if I'm in that kind of a basket case [incompetent], I don't care whether it's my wife, my son, or my daughter making the decisions or facing the issues if they're capable, and at this point they are. That's why I wrote whom I did down. It's my wife and saving her, my son, and then on down with my other two daughters after that. And I guess my wife isn't as logical, but after that all three children are equally competent I would say. They are all in the city, but who knows where one of them might be at a given point of emergency, and so the advice was to always have other alternates." Another participant discussed how her husband had made his decisions about appointing agents. "My husband had appointed myself and if I wasn't able to, then it would have been my son. Personally we spoke about it that our son would, of course, speak to his sisters. One is, like our little one, the one who is going through the divorce, she is quite emotional, and she takes things a little [harder]. And the other one was expecting a baby so we didn't want to put the burden on them. BUT it was understood that they would have a discussion. The girls definitely were not gonna be kept out of it or in the dark. But our son was to make the definite arrangements. That was only if I wasn't capable."

Although most participants had identified someone to be responsible for making decisions for them should they become incompetent, they did not want them to bear any legal or other consequences for making decisions on their behalf. One participant stated, "We [husband and wife] absolved them [their children] of any liability in making these decisions. That may bother some people; it doesn't me." In her written directive, another participant wrote, "I recognize that this appears to place a heavy responsibility upon you [her agents], but this directive is made with the intention of relieving you of such responsibility and placing it upon myself in accordance with my strong conviction. I hereby absolve my physician or any physician taking care of me, from any legal liability pertaining to the performance of my requests and demands." To date, there have been no legal challenges to the *Personal Directives Act* in Alberta, so the legal strength of these clauses remains untested.

In a large Canadian study of outpatients of all ages, patients indicated that they were most likely to have discussed their preferences for life-sustaining treatment with friends first, then spouses and children (Sam & Singer, 1993). Interestingly, when selecting a substitute decision-maker, the order shifted—individuals were most likely to choose spouses, children, and then friends. The observation that one is most likely to talk about these kinds of decisions with friends, but least likely to select them as surrogates, is a perplexing phenomenon. Perhaps the dialogue between friends is a less threatening place to test out ideas so that later discussions with a spouse and/ or children proceed more smoothly. This would be akin to a dress rehearsal where one has the opportunity to work out some of the finer details and make adjustments before the curtain is raised on opening night. Scott-Maxwell (1968), an 83-year-old woman, writer, and Jungian psychologist describes her discussions about death with a good friend this way: "With one friend of my own age we cheerfully exchange the worst symptoms, and our black dreads as well. We frequently talk of death, for we are very alert to the experience of the unknown that may be so near and it is only to those of one's own age that one can speak frankly" (p. 31).

Many individuals in the study I conducted did talk to friends during the process of preparing a directive, but it wasn't evident if these discussions took place before conversations with family. Only one participant named a friend, who also happened to be a nurse, as her sole agent. In selecting a nurse, this participant believed she was choosing someone who was knowledgeable about end-of-life issues. She said, "As a matter of fact, the agent that I have chosen is a nurse and certainly deals with end-of-life VERY often. And so she gave me all of the possible scenarios, about if you're this way they'll do such and such, and if you're this way they'll do something else, and whatever, whatever...I am leaving that [decisions about my end-of-life such as stopping life-sustaining treatment] up to my friend who is certainly more qualified than any of my children to assess my situation. I definitely knew that I didn't want my children to have to say 'pull the plug' and then feel guilty about it. She was my best choice, I believe."

Another participant named a family member and a friend. In preparing her advance directive, this participant consulted a lawyer. She said, "I wouldn't have thought of choosing somebody if it hadn't been for the lawyer. That's one thing. My sister was my first choice. And I know that she would abide by my wishes and that's partly because that's part of the family values that we have, that everybody makes their own decisions, people don't make decisions for somebody else. The other person I chose, and I know she would be faithful and would make herself available, is a friend."

Participants were also clear about the persons that they did not want to be their substitute decision-makers. One participant stated, "We have some more distant relatives that I would cringe to think about appointing as an agent because of their inability to face some serious issues in life, especially life and death." Isobel, Alice's friend referred to earlier, chose not to select her children as her agents because she did not want them to be in the difficult position of making end-of-life decisions for her. She believed her friend who was a nurse and had breast cancer was better equipped and intuitively more able to make such decisions. In Isobel's words, her friend "can empathize with every single feeling that I have...and understands completely." One participant had reservations about choosing a good friend, because she had recently witnessed her friend having difficulty in dealing with life-sustaining decisions about her own mother's death. This participant believes her friend's mother underwent some invasive tests and procedures that were unnecessary and unwanted, and she wonders if this friend would be a strong advocate for her. This same participant had thought about naming a husband and wife as her agents, but her lawyer advised against this because of the possibility that the couple might at some point become separated or divorced. The lawyer explained that a potential situation of conflict could arise and that her interests could get caught in the middle. Another participant thought it was important to select someone who was younger because "someone younger, really, can cope with it better, too. Like...as you get older you can't cope with stuff, you shouldn't have to, you know...It's hard enough to look after yourself as you get older without having to look after other people." Ironically, this participant is an agent for two friends who are only a few years her elder.

Earlier I discussed how the term "agent" seemed to lack any notion of relationship, that it was a rather cold and business-like term. During our conversations, participants talked about their agent's duty to respect their wishes. This sense of duty, however, seemed to stem from the relationship the agent had with the participant rather than from the signing of a legal document. The notion of relationship was important throughout the process of naming, selecting, and trusting an agent to act on their behalf. No one selected a stranger or employed a paid professional (such as a lawyer or doctor) to be their substitute decision-maker. Because of the educational material they had accessed, participants were familiar with and used the term "agent" often in our conversations. There was a sense that their agents would be close by, ready, and willing to do battle.

trusting your agent

I am so fortunate to have three children who are available to go to bat for me whenever I need them. When I visualize myself incapable, I picture three warriors who will do the best they can. I trust them with that. I believe that if I didn't trust them, the whole idea—the whole directive— would be futile. I have to accept that they will do what I want. I can't imagine what it is like for someone like my husband's friend, John, to have nobody he can trust to make decisions for him. He is relying solely on the piece of paper he has signed to be his spokesperson to relay his last wishes. He hopes that his advance directive ends up in good hands, the right hands.

Selecting an agent, indeed the entire process of preparing an advance directive, seems to revolve around the concepts of trust and fidelity. Fidelity "addresses issues of mutual faithfulness between individuals…Under the principle of fidelity, one is held to the promises that one makes" (Winters, Glass, & Sakurai, 1993, p. 22). Study participants said they trust their agents to make decisions in accordance with their wishes if there are no written directions for a specific situation. Participants trust that the documents will be provided to relevant decision-makers. Participants also trust that health professionals will act in accordance with their written instructions. Only one participant did not name an agent. His decision reflected his independent lifestyle and the fact that he was not close to most of his family members. This preference for independent decision-making is identified in the literature (Sam & Singer, 1993). The literature does note that a reason for not selecting an agent is the lack of a suitable person within one's sphere of relationships (Sam & Singer, 1993).

Participants expressed confidence in their agents to make the decisions that were in their best interests. When I asked one participant if she had any concerns that she might change her mind about what she wanted if she were to become incapacitated, she said, "I think I've left a good margin of variation there. But, again, I would have to put my trust in the agent, in consultation with the doctor, to know whether I am still as lucid as I want to be. You know. Is it the pain that's talking or is it the bottom line? There are so many variables, depending on the degree of demise, I guess. It would be up to the agents to know whether I am making the right decisions or not, if I start changing my mind, if I say, 'Go ahead, break my ribs!' or whatever." Another participant was certain that her wishes would be followed. "I know that my daughter, the one that's away. She'd come down here like a thundercloud if she thought they weren't doing [what I wanted]. Oh yeah, oh yeah, she would come down and say, 'Look! Every one of those things has to be carried out! THAT'S mother's wishes.' Yeah, oh yeah, she's very, very much aware that people's wishes should be carried out. She's very aware that this is how I feel." Another participant, based on her agent's history, expressed her confidence this way, "She's been through this with her own dad, and if she can make those decisions for her dad, she can make them for me."

In discussing the trust he placed in his agents to follow his directions and advocate on his behalf, one participant told the story of a situation in which his advance directive had already been used. He said, "I know after discussing with my children that my daughters wouldn't have any hesitation of acting on my behalf, too, and supporting her [his wife]…[If a situation were to arise they would be able to say] 'I don't want you to touch him! Leave him alone, he doesn't want you to touch him, so leave him alone.' As a matter of fact, when I went in the hospital this time and I was in respiratory arrest, my daughter made damned sure [they knew about my directive]…She went out and checked the chart and made sure it's [the directive] on there. You know, and so I don't have that kind of worry."

In preparing an advance directive, there is an ongoing tension between the notions of trust and distrust. As defined in the dictionary, to trust means "to have or place confidence in" (Webster, 1984, p. 736). In making the decision to prepare an advance directive, one is in many ways acknowledging a distrust of the healthcare system, of healthcare providers, perhaps even of family members. We are not confident that they will make decisions consistent with how we want to be cared for. Paradoxically, however, in preparing an advance directive we trust that others will respect our written wishes. In choosing an individual to act as our substitute decision-maker, we are explicitly placing our trust in them to carry out our wishes.

In my conversations with participants about naming and selecting an agent, I began to consider who I would trust to make decisions on my behalf. Who do I want to include in that decision-making process? Who would I exclude? Is trust the overriding consideration in selecting a substitute decision-maker? Selecting an agent is not necessarily an easy task. How can the process of choosing an ally be facilitated?

getting
IT DONE

5

Reflection on death has taught me that fulfillment in life can only come from defining clearly what we want before death.

(Kavanagh, 1972, p. 17)

gathering information

The morning after the information session, I began the process of completing my own directive. The Alberta government produced a series of pamphlets with information about advance directives, so I phoned the number the lawyer had given us and ordered my free copy. Although there were many ideas running through my mind, I didn't start putting anything on paper right away. I waited until I had a chance to review the pamphlets. I also wanted to touch base with my family doctor about my own health status. Although I am pretty healthy now, I have had the occasional angina attack (my dad died of a heart attack as did several of his brothers and sisters), so I wanted to talk to her about the most likely scenarios given my own and my family's history. I'd also been keeping my eyes peeled for articles in the daily paper and in the senior's publications that I receive. So far, I had clipped out a few and tucked them away in a file clearly labelled: AD/AD—Alice Dawson/Advance Directive.

Several weeks went by. My package from the government arrived. I was anxious to get started, so I skimmed through the materials quickly. There was one pamphlet that talked specifically about how to prepare my own directive. "Choosing Now for the Future" the title loudly proclaimed. I retreated to my favourite reading chair with a cup of green tea to read it more carefully. It provided the bare bones of what should be contained in a written directive and gave a lot of information about points to consider. It quickly became apparent, though, that I would have to do most of the writing myself. I guess I was hoping there would be a template, and all I would have to do was fill in my name. But that would be too easy, *wouldn't it? After all, everyone has different ideas about how we want our life and death to unfold. It's probably a good thing there was room for personalizing my directive. If we all wanted the same type of treatment at the end-of-life, we wouldn't need advance directives, would we?*

Alice is a practical, organized person and has been thorough in her approach to completing a directive. This thoughtfulness was evident with most of the participants of the study I conducted. This chapter describes how older adults moved from considering preparing an advance directive to actually completing one. In the literature, surprisingly little is written about this aspect of advance directives. Consequently, it is the experiences of the older adults in my study that dominate this discussion.

Participants gathered information about advance directives primarily through three avenues—reading written materials, attending public seminars, and consulting one-on-one with various individuals.

READING MATERIALS
Participants obtained written information about advance directives from a variety of sources: the government, bookstores, neighbours, and the Internet. In conjunction with the enactment of the *Personal Directives Act*, the Government of Alberta prepared the set of brochures that Alice refers to as part of a public education program. A number of study participants had obtained these brochures, entitled "Choosing Now for the Future," which included a guide to writing a personal directive, a description of the responsibilities of service providers under the *Personal Directives Act*, and an explanation of the duties and obligations of an agent. One participant recalled, "The priest here asked me if I would help look after funerals and, you know, talk with the people and help prepare and then be there at the funeral. And I did this for two years. And during this time it came to my attention that there was a lot of grief [conflict as to what should be done such as burial versus cremation] that wasn't necessary for the families. And the whole idea of personal directives was just new, what four years ago, five years ago, and I sent for the books." Another participant said, "I'd thought a lot about a directive even before it was called a personal directive, when they called them living wills.

But it just seemed so nebulous until the Government made the Act ongoing...it took me quite a while to gather the material. I looked in so many places."

ATTENDING SEMINARS

Alternatively or in addition to gathering and reading information about advance directives, a number of individuals attended educational sessions about end-of-life advance care planning. According to one participant, "The senior citizens group brought a lawyer in. For the life of me, I can't remember his name. I do know he was a lawyer and he was excellent, and I took copious notes. Both my wife and I went. We came home and we followed the instructions he had laid out, and he said you can see a lawyer or you can do it on your own. So we decided to make a living will on our own. And we pretty well followed everything that the lawyer had told us. He gave us the bare bones; it was a skeleton. We didn't copy it from anything; we just did it on our own." Another participant said, "I attended a few sessions at different places. I think one was put on by the Good Samaritan Society. I attended that and then we had people come and talk to us. I say we, the church. We also had someone come and talk about inexpensive funerals."

Another participant indicated that she "went to various seminars. There was a whole evening there and they had literature and handouts and everything and that was kind of my start and then I went to, maybe, another couple of seminars that I obviously can't remember, where they had a whole sheaf of paper!" During her nursing career, one participant indicated that she went to seminars on topics related to end-of-life, but not specifically to any about preparing an advance directive. She said, "I went to a lecture that was put on by the law faculty on euthanasia and so they were talking about euthanasia and sort of clarified to me the difference between legally killing somebody and prolonging their dying, and so that was useful, too. And, probably, one of the things that was the MOST helpful was I went to a workshop on death and dying. And the person who did the workshop had done a lot of work with Kübler-Ross [an expert who has published widely in the area of death and dying]."

Around the time of the enactment of the legislation in Alberta, there were public education seminars about advance directives put on by various organizations and individuals, including a number by Alberta's Office of the Public Guardian, which continues to offer workshops today.

CONSULTING OTHERS

Some participants consulted with others, experts and non-experts, prior to, during, and after completing their own directives. Lawyers were most often consulted for expert advice on the legal aspects of preparing an advance directive. One participant stated, "It didn't appear to be something I wished to fill out on my own. I wasn't sure of the wording or anything, so my financial advisor has a number of other professionals that he calls on for various things and he suggested a lawyer whom I went to and had one made up." Several also conferred with religious advisors and friends. One participant recalled, "I went for a walk with a friend and we talked about it. But making the decisions wasn't hard, handling the emotions that were associated with it—that was the hard part, to keep my emotions out of my thinking. And then when I finally did go to a lawyer, talking with him was really very therapeutic. And he wrote a beautiful living will and said it much better than I think I had. When I went back and read it over, he asked if he had captured it [what I wanted] and he had done it even better than I could have."

Another participant indicated, "I immediately got hold of some of the forms and went through them and discussed them with my minister at the time, and he was the one that had signed my first living will. And that would have been many years ago, here and gone. I guess, it would be almost 20 years ago when I did my first living will or whenever they came out. And I have not changed my mind in any way about my future, and the older I get the more I am convinced that I do not want to prolong my life by any of the new gizmos that they come up with. I mean they're coming up with things all along and they have all these replacements. I do not feel that I want to be kept alive through a whole lot of medical intervention, I just don't feel that way about my life."

One participant, along with his wife, consulted with an individual from Alberta's Office of the Public Guardian. In describing his interaction with this individual the participant said, "She's very, very personable and just full of stories, and I guess one of the most knowledgeable people in Alberta in this area. She has lots of stories to tell about what happens if you don't have good planning of a personal directive in place. She gave us each about 20 minutes of personal one-on-one time to fine tune what we had developed from all the written material and forms and guidelines that she'd given us. She has her own guideline called 'Workshop on Making a Personal Directive: It's More Than a Living Will.'" Others hesitated to consult individuals outside the family. One participant stated, "I guess I'm more of the old school of taking care of yourself and doing what's necessary and only bringing one of the so-called experts when you need to, as a last resort almost in some cases." Another said, "I just didn't see any point in involving a lawyer for something if it's not necessary."

As participants talked about how they gathered information about advance directives, it seemed that serendipity played a significant role in their access to information. Coming into contact with key individuals and resources appeared to happen somewhat by accident. I wondered about the many seniors who have fewer resources and more limited access to information. Do they have the same opportunity to consider, plan, and control what happens to them at the end-of-life? Do advance directives represent another instance of discrimination? I was also struck by how several participants indicated that they tried to keep emotion out of the decision-making process. I found this somewhat ironic. Life and death situations are among the most emotional that one can encounter, yet there was a desire to suppress the expression of emotions. Why are we so uncomfortable in acknowledging emotion? How can we embrace and incorporate emotion into our end-of-life decision-making?

personalizing the data

During my annual physical examination, I mentioned to my doctor that I was completing a directive. She thought it was a good idea. Our discussion about it was short—she was already at least an hour behind in her appointments. But basically she said given my history of heart disease, the potential for me to have a heart attack was definitely there. The statistics she shared with me about CPR (cardiopulmonary resuscitation) were pretty grim. So, one of the things I've included in my written directive is I do not want to be resuscitated. I actually think a quick death by a massive heart attack would be a good way to go; it would be even better if it happened silently in my sleep.

My doctor also said, given my age, it was unlikely many of my organs would be in good enough shape to be donated, but I've stated anyway that I am willing to donate any usable organs. I wouldn't have any further use for them, so this seems like a reasonable gesture. I've also been toying with donating my body to science, but I haven't made a decision about that yet. I think the idea is a good one, yet I can't get past the thought of young men and women standing over my body and dissecting it.

After gathering general information about advance directives, participants integrated the information into their own personal situations. One participant with a history of breast cancer had a discussion with her doctor about her prognosis. She described her conversation with her doctor like this: "Yeah, I definitely asked her, you know, on a scale of one to ten what are my chances, where do I sit on that scale if ten would be the best outcome? And she told me about a four. So I said, 'Wow! That's not very good!' And she said, 'Well, you asked.' So then we had further discussion." This same participant also asked one of her friends who was a nurse for detailed information about possible end-of-life scenarios. "I just sat her down and said, 'I want you to tell me all about this and I want you to tell me what will happen if my heart stops or, you know, I can't recollect everything.' But we went through it considerably."

Another participant also had a discussion with a friend who was a nurse. "She gave me a form and asked me to write my impressions down and then we discussed them. There was tube feeding and there was intravenous. There were all three: air, food, and hydration. We talked about hydration quite a bit. And I, you know, we talked about how inhumane it was if somebody was thirsty not to give them a drink." Yet another participant recalled, "I had some ideas of my own. If I were so ill that it seemed unlikely that I could recover or at least recover completely mentally, then I wouldn't want all the ICU things done that would save me. And also I felt strongly that my children shouldn't feel obliged to keep me in their own home if I were unable to live on my own. If it came to that, there are public and private facilities, (pause) but I hope they come and visit me."

Several participants had the perception that their physicians and other healthcare providers were too busy to take time for lengthy discussions about the future. One participant stated, "I just handed it to him [the doctor], he was very busy, I'm sure he's filed it and read it, he knows how I feel." Another participant, speaking of a recent hospitalization, said, "I'm just thinking how busy they were. They had trouble looking after just the physical needs." This perception may be another reason older adults rarely initiate discussions about end-of-life with their physicians and other health professionals. Are health professionals really too busy to talk about important life and death issues? Or is busyness an avoidance strategy—a convenient barrier that limits conversations about death?

One of the personal decisions that a number of participants struggled with was the issue of organ donation. Within the Alberta legislation, agents do not have the authority to make determinations about removal of tissue from a living body. So, if individuals were willing to donate an organ (such as a kidney to one of their children), it must be specifically and clearly stated within their written directive. For one participant, it was during the preparation of his advance directive that he was stimulated to consider donating his organs. He said, "I've got an organ donor authorization here [in his directive]. That particular section I had never really confronted before. And it took a little talking with my wife as to whether we should do it and why and so on and so forth, but we've gone ahead with it. But certainly when you think of agreeing to cornea transplants and other organs, it's not pleasant, but, you know, it's something you can face. You don't have to put it in if you don't want to but we did...If one of my family needs a kidney and I'm still around and it's compatible, I've given them the okay to do that."

Another participant indicated that organ donation had been discussed in her family previously. She said, "We'd have the discussion on donating organs if it came on the news, 'cause we'd listened to the news as we were eating our supper. And so we were always very open in these situations. And because it's easier as the time comes, everybody knows what to be prepared for. The children are used to knowing that if something happened to Mom and Dad, say that it was at the point where the organs would be used or whatever, it's not a surprise to them." Expressing his opinion on organ donation, one participant said, "Everybody should, if they can, donate their organs if they die. I can't, because medically my organs are shot. But to me this is what you do. You've got your organ donor card, you sign that, you've got the directive, you sign that, you've got your wallet. Then your family knows what's to happen." One individual had decided to donate her body to science saying, "I have been obese all my life, and if by taking my body apart they could find something that caused this—perhaps there is research that could be done." For the older adult, organ donation is a phenomenon that did not exist during their childhood or early adult years. Does this impact their awareness or understanding of the process of organ donation? Do many think they are too old—that none of their organs would be of value? Should organ donation be addressed separately, outside of the context of an advance directive? Is it perhaps lost among the many other end-of-life decisions that can be addressed in an advance directive?

Despite being an aspect of preparing an advance directive, only a few participants pursued obtaining specific information about their own health status and the most likely scenarios they might encounter because of their past medical history. Singer (1995) suggests this is a role for the person's own doctor. He suggests, "In his or her role as health educator, the doctor may raise the issue of advance care planning with his or her patients...and direct the patient to the appropriate tools to support the process. The doctor could also tailor the information about health states and treatments to the person's own particular health situation" (pp. 6–7). How can older adults and their physicians be encouraged and supported to engage in such discussions?

writing and rewriting

Although I'm a novice, I have been enjoying learning how to use the computer. So, I figured typing up my directive was a good opportunity to practice my word-processing skills. This way I can easily access the document, make changes, and print copies whenever I need to.

My directive has evolved over time and now has three sections. In the first section, I have included my personal statement of values. In the second, I have included written directions. And in the third, I have named my agents. Although the first section is only a little more than a page in length, it took me forever to write it (and that had nothing to do with my pathetic typing speed). I'd keep going back, changing a few things, setting it aside for a few days (sometimes weeks), and then rereading and rewriting some more, until it felt right. It was time consuming and emotional at times, too. On more than one occasion, I had to stop typing because tears blurred my vision. Preparing my directive made me think about my husband and his death. How can I explain to you what it felt like to lose my best friend, the love of my life, the father of my children? The pain is sometimes unbearable. Then I would take a few deep breaths, the anguish would pass, and I would carry on.

For my personal statement of values, it was a challenge to sum up what I am all about in just a page or two, but I persevered. Let me read to you the first paragraph:

> I have tried to live my life with dignity, and I need to be allowed to die the same way. Death, to me, is a reality as much as birth, growth, maturity, and old age. I think of death as life's greatest adventure! If I am faced with an endlessly painful demise, please keep me comfortable even if it shortens my life. I need to die with dignity, without inflicting prolonged distress on my children or, indeed, myself!

I think you get the gist of my thoughts on life and death and what I believe is important. I think you have to put some thought into writing your own personal statement, to express your feelings—this may be the most important step in writing your directive.

When it came to deciding what to include in their directives, participants used a variety of approaches ranging from one individual who simply signed a living will form he purchased at a bookstore, to others who spent hours, days, and weeks revising the content. Appendix B presents a sample advance directive representing the type of content most participants included. The appointment of an agent, information about how and when the directive comes into effect, the powers of the agent, personal decisions, and access to documents and information were topics frequently addressed in the directives. One participant said the following about preparing her personal statement of values: "I wrote and I wrote (laughs), and I wrote and I crossed out and I changed and I did this and I did that and it took me, probably, weeks." Some individuals included specific individualized instructions in their directives. For instance, one participant had family members who were alternative therapy practitioners (such as Reiki). Because of her religious beliefs, this participant was adamant that she did not want to be the recipient of any of these alternative modalities. She said, "I have that quite detailed in my personal directive, because he [her agent] would not be able to control [the actions of] the rest of the family members without proof that it's what I want."

Several expressed satisfaction in the process of authoring their own advance directives. One said, "I did this myself. I have it on my word processor. The doctor and lawyer seemed to think that it was okay. He [the lawyer] never changed it. He used what I had written." Within the context of advance directives, there is a parallel that can be drawn between the terms "author" as a writer or the originator of an event, and "authority" as the power or right to enforce obedience (Barber, 2001). In authoring their advance directives, individuals are exercising their autonomy and legal and moral right to control what happens to them. Given the potentially significant outcomes related to enacting an advance directive, one operates on the assumption that the statements reflect the thoughts of a well-informed author. But how do we know that the author was properly informed?

I think back to one of my own attempts at authoring my personal directive. I retrieve from my burgeoning file of information another example of an advance directive. Maybe it will capture the essence of what I want to tell the world about the way that I want my life before death to unfold. Maybe.

> I, _____ , being of sound mind, make known my wishes. If the time comes when I can no longer take part in decisions for my future, I have chosen one or more option(s) as indicated by my initials. If I have an incurable condition, as determined by two or more physicians:

_____ 1. I direct that I be allowed to die naturally without medical intervention.

_____ 2. I direct that I be allowed to die with comfort measures such as nursing care and relief of pain.

_____ 3. I request neither cardiopulmonary resuscitation nor admission to an intensive care unit.

_____ 4. I request to live my last days at home rather than in a hospital if this is agreeable with my family.

_____ 5. I donate any of my tissues that are of value for transplants.

_____ 6. Other

These statements are made after careful consideration and are in accordance with my strong convictions and beliefs. I have asked _____ to be my healthcare agent to make treatment decisions on my behalf. This permission shall remain effective in the event that I become incompetent or unable to make decisions for myself. If my healthcare agent is unavailable, another person will be identified in accordance with local legislation.

This template seems pretty straightforward. All I have to do is put my initials beside the statements I agree with. I read the first one: I direct that I be allowed to die naturally without medical intervention. What exactly does this mean? What is a natural death? The only natural death that I can think of is one that occurs as a result of old age, where your heart just tires out and you die quietly in your sleep. But I am not old, at least not that old. And if I die in my sleep, I will not need an advance directive. I go on to number two: I direct that I be allowed to die with comfort measures such as nursing care and relief of pain. Is nursing care always a comfort measure? How do I explain the grimaces of pain on the patient's face that I as a nurse witnessed as I slowly turned her from side to side to prevent the development of pressure sores? How do I explain to a young boy that this injection that causes him to hurt is necessary?

I scan down the list to number four: I request to live my last days at home rather than in a hospital if this is agreeable with my family. Yes, I think I'd rather die in familiar surroundings than in a cold, sterile hospital room, but what if that would cause hardship for my family? Would I expect them to put their lives on hold to care for me on my deathbed? The answers are not clear to me. The written words of others do not adequately reflect how I want my life before death to transpire. I will have to use my own words. But I am too tired now and my head is aching; I cannot think about this anymore today. I close the document, not even bothering to save what I have typed. I will try again tomorrow. But tomorrow never seems to come. How is it that this day has arrived for others? It was only when I was faced with surgery, several years later, that I was finally able to complete the task of writing my own advance directive.

Historically, there have been many rituals associated with death and dying. Over time, many of these rituals have disappeared, because many people are no longer affiliated with a religious faith (Anderson, 2001). According to Anderson (2001), "Rituals have the ability to bring people an experience of something greater. They create a safe space and time in which we can touch the deeper issues of our existence. They have the power to bring to the surface and resolve very deep feelings and unnamed blocks that have been buried in our unconscious" (p. 40). For the participants in my study, advance directives seem to have allowed participants to look inside themselves and to reflect upon some of life's greatest questions. Is it possible that preparing an advance directive is an end-of-life ritual for the twenty-first century?

keeping it simple

I've kept my written directions fairly simple and brief, because I don't want my children to be bound too tightly by what I've written. For example, although I don't want to have a feeding tube, I haven't written that down because a situation might arise where I would fully recover if one were used for a short time. But my children know that, under most circumstances, I do not want a feeding tube.

Based on my conversation with my doctor, I have included a statement that I do not want to receive cardiopulmonary resuscitation if my heart stops beating as a result of heart disease or some other traumatic event. I have also indicated that I do want to receive pain medication and other comfort measures so that I can die as peacefully and pain free as possible. If I have a treatable condition (like a broken hip or pneumonia), and there

is a good possibility that I will be restored to my previous health in a rela-
tively short time, I do want to receive the full range of possible treatments
(including hospitalization, surgery, or antibiotics).

One of the things we talked about a lot at our family meeting was the
kind of treatment I would want if I were terminally ill. There's no question
that if the prognosis is grim, I don't want to be a burden on the system or
my family. In that situation, the less attempts at heroics, the better. So, I've
included the statement: "If I am terminally ill and, in the opinion of my
physician and other consultants, have no known hope of cure, I do not wish
my life to be prolonged by artificial means." As I mentioned before, I've
also included a statement about donating any usable organs.

While writing my advance directive, I constantly asked myself, "Does
each statement do what I want it to do? Will it perform the way I want it
to perform?"

Study participants sought to make their directives straightforward and simple. One participant stated, "The main directive
is pretty basic but areas like 'do not resuscitate' and what type of
accommodation I would like and all that, we didn't put that down in
the directive because we were advised not to for a number of reasons.
That's the simplicity of our document." Another participant referred
to her neighbour's directive as she completed her own. This participant said, "She gave me some of the stuff that she'd completed and
I just sort of looked at that and whatnot. But mine just is a one-page
thing and it just states my agent and that's it. I haven't gone beyond
that...I think one of the reasons I've kept it simple at this stage is I
don't feel I'm going to need it for a while yet, you know, and it's subject to change." Another participant tried to keep the language she
used simple and clear. She said, "It's not written out in any scientific
way but, to me, my statement is adamant enough and my agent
knows me well enough and knows any situation that could arise."
Keeping it simple is another of the paradoxes about advance directives. How can a document that purports to describe how one's death
and dying is to unfold in any way be construed as simple?

following the rules

I thought about taking my advance directive to my lawyer to have him
review it, but in the end I was satisfied that I had followed all of the

regulations. I didn't see any sense in spending money if it wasn't required. Actually, I think that the ability to complete an advance directive without legal counsel is great, especially for seniors on a limited budget. It means that anyone can complete a directive; it's not limited to only those with the necessary financial resources. If you want to do it, there really is no excuse not to complete a directive.

Unlike Alice, some participants were concerned that their directives might not conform to the legal requirements and so they included a lawyer in the process. One participant said, "So after we did decide [to prepare a directive] I contacted my lawyer and I, you know, had it prepared, these documents. And, you know, once they were prepared and signed I gave each of my children a copy." Another participant stated, "I let the lawyer tend to the necessary tickety-boo stuff, but I wrote a personal statement that expresses my feelings, my wishes, and how I want to be taken care of if I become terminal... I had asked him initially, 'Essentially what has to be in a directive?' and he said, 'The best thing for you to do is to make your personal statement,' he says, 'so that it's very clear as to what your wishes are and you're not waffling around.' And if you want non-care to a certain degree or whatever, you have to make your thoughts known. So this is what I hope I've done."

Having a lawyer involved gave some participants a sense of security. One participant stated, "I felt very secure knowing that this was the newer and officially acceptable way of having my wishes being put, you know, put to paper and signed. So I felt much more secure knowing that this was something that the government had initiated and would accept." Several participants considered completing their advance directive as part of a package of documents required to adequately prepare for end-of-life that included estate wills and power of attorney for property. One participant reported, "When we went to have our wills updated, we asked him about the living will. He said it was called a personal directive. And he did it, it's very simple, simple rules, we more or less told him what we want, like not prolonging life, that we want to be comfortable. And so we had that done. Not hoping we would have to use it, but we did, and it was very helpful and very comforting not only for me but for our son."

reflecting on the process

I remember when I finished composing my directive, including my personal statement of values. It was long past dusk on a cool November evening when I finally printed a copy and shut down the computer. I felt great! It was done and on paper. The relief was just like what a person feels once her estate will is finally drawn up.

It took me more than eight months to write my directive. I remember thinking at the information session that this would be a simple task for an afternoon or evening. I was a bit off on that prediction! I found it was a process that couldn't be rushed. I needed time to gather information and facts, to talk to my children, to talk to my family doctor, to write and rewrite, and perhaps most importantly of all to sit quietly, think, and reflect. Now, there were just a few minor housekeeping items to attend to, such as making and distributing copies to my children, my family doctor, my minister, and my lawyer.

During the study I conducted, one of the topics that we discussed was how participants felt upon completion of their directives. One of the most frequent responses was simply relief that "it's done." One participant said, "What struck me was once it's done, that's it." Another said, "That's what I want and I'm happy about it, that it's done...Yeah, that's right, I don't have to prepare any more, it's done, yeah." Another common response of participants was that completing an advance directive provided them with a sense of comfort. One participant said, "It just made me feel great. I really feel comfortable and pleased that we had it all done. Yeah. Actually, yes, I guess you could say security. Because particularly at that time I was running into another operation and that, our wills were done, my directive was there and I went into the operation feeling, 'Well, I've done everything I can, now they do what they can, if they can't do it that's fine.' You know, I don't know what happens after you're dead but that's it, you know. So I felt very comfortable, very comfortable." Another common response was that it made participants feel good, positive. "Yeah, it made me feel positive that I had taken care of myself and my own wishes, while I am still competent to make those decisions," said one participant. Another said, "I felt good. This was the way I wanted the world to unfold in the future and it was down on paper now and they'd better not ignore it."

In reflecting on the process of completing a directive, one participant remarked, "Initially you think the directive is a simple thing. You just write down, 'I don't want to be resuscitated, don't do a damned thing, okay.'" Another expressed, "I think you have to put some thought into it. And I think you have to express your feelings and make that personal statement. I think that personal statement is the most important thing of the whole business." Yet another said of the process, "It was an interesting one. You know, being able to do it, to try to think about what things would be."

There is the suggestion in the literature that "participating in discussions about personal goals about future care may alleviate some of the frightening uncertainties related to the disease and the patient's prognosis" (Neumark, 1994, p. 771). Additionally, one author states that "involvement in choice-of-care decisions is critical to many patients for whom maintaining a sense of control is vital to their quality of life" (Griffin, 1993, p. 39). In the quotation by Kavanagh (1972) that opens this chapter, he suggests that defining what we want to happen prior to our death is a prerequisite to a fulfilling life. Most participants expressed an unwavering certainty about controlling how their end-of-life would unfold, something that is inherently uncertain. Another paradox is that the completion of an advance directive as an expression of one's autonomy cannot be done autonomously. If one does not involve others, at least to the extent of informing them that a directive exists, where it is located, and its contents, there is no mechanism for the individual's wishes to be respected.

Preparing one's advance directive is a relatively unique experience. There are few situations in which we consider our wishes for our projected future selves in such a systematic manner. Additionally, there are few undertakings that have the potential to impact one's life and death in such a permanent and personal way. Completing an estate will is somewhat similar in that one must face his or her mortality, but differs in that it is only enacted after the death of the maker. As well, its impact is felt only on those left behind and does not directly affect the maker. Planning for retirement also has some similarities. In planning for their financial security, individuals take into consideration their values and priorities in life. However, it does not necessarily require people to confront their own mortality in such a direct way. Advance directives require individuals to do both—face their own mortality and imagine their future and responses to unforeseen situations. Are these demands humanly possible? Perhaps it is because both of these tasks are difficult, if not impossible for many, that the completion rate of advance directives is relatively low.

Can completing an advance directive really put one's mind at rest about one's pending death? Is this a false sense of closure, wishful thinking? Maybe. Are there any guarantees that preparing a directive will help one to die well? Perhaps not. But does it really matter? Could it be that the process of preparing an advance directive is more important, more meaningful, more comforting than the actual outcome of a death that precisely mirrors one's prospective wishes? Perhaps it is the opportunity to reflect on one's life and to share those reflections with family and friends that is of ultimate value and significance. Perhaps completing an advance directive is more about living well than dying well.

looking toward the future

I know many people who attended the session at the church haven't written their own directives yet. I think this is unfortunate. What convinced me to do it, I think, were the compelling stories about what can happen if you don't have good planning in place. I'd be naïve if I thought completing an advance directive would guarantee that I will be able to control everything that happens to me. And that's okay. Although my directive is important to me, it's probably even more important to my children. I want to make things as straightforward as possible for them. I want them to be comfortable. I don't want them to face unnecessary challenges at a time that is already challenging enough.

I think completing a directive has improved my life in ways I'd never expected. It brought me face to face with my own mortality. Hopefully it will make the days I have left more valuable and better lived—and relationships better treasured than they might have otherwise been. I look forward with great anticipation to my future, from receiving a bouquet of dandelions freshly picked by my youngest granddaughter, to learning the steps to the latest line dance.

As our conversations drew to a close, I often asked participants if they had any closing thoughts about their experience of preparing an advance directive. On a number of occasions, they had a message of encouragement for others to "get it done." One participant said, "I think everyone should have a directive and even the young people who are invincible, you know. Because what you really want is not always discussed as much as it should be." Another who had completed his directive shortly after finding out about their existence said, "I haven't been putting this off because we just discovered it and did it, but if people do know about personal directives and aren't doing it, I think they're dragging their feet." Still another said, "I think everybody should know about it and everybody should discuss it with their children or if they don't have children, their partner, or if they don't have a partner, a very close friend. And if they're lacking all of that then their minister if they're religious, and if they're not I kind of figure, their lawyer otherwise (laughs). But I feel that everybody should give some thought to their final days and what condition they might be in during those final days and what they would like to happen to them should they not be able to say it then."

How can we help others to get it done? How can we help ourselves to get it done?

closing
THOUGHTS

Conclusion

We no longer completely trust the system or the professionals who handled our end-of-life dilemmas…We have lost sight of how life could, and should, end. It is time to give back to our dying a human, or a humanly understandable, face.

(Ahronheim & Weber, 1992, pp. 14, 27)

reconsidering expectations

Since I first began conceptualizing this research project, there have
been several studies completed and papers published suggesting that
advance directives have failed to live up to their original expectations (for example, Ditto et al., 2001; Prendergast, 2001; Teno, Lynn et
al., 1997). At the time of their introduction, advance directives were
considered by many to be a panacea for resolving end-of-life decision-
making dilemmas that were occurring on an increasingly frequent
basis. New life-sustaining technologies, along with rising healthcare
costs, an aging population, raised consumer awareness about health
matters, and increasing healthcare litigation were among the factors contributing to this situation. It was thought that preparing a
directive would ensure appropriate and individualized end-of-life
treatment and care. It was also thought that everyone, once they were
informed about advance directives, would immediately sit down
and prepare one. Advance directives were expected to be financially
advantageous as they would result in significant cost-savings for the
healthcare system.

The introduction of advance directives has not consistently met all
of these lofty goals. However, the analysis and interpretation of the
data in my study leads me to suggest that despite these disappointing
outcomes, there are distinct and tangible benefits to completing an
advance directive, some of which have not been adequately appreci-
ated or examined. The study findings also provide insight as to why
some approaches to implementing advance directives (for example,
having a stranger initiate the discussion; introducing the subject at

the time of admission to hospital) have been relatively ineffective at increasing completion rates of advance directives, or more importantly, improving end-of-life care. These strategies do not take into account the need for ongoing conversations and the importance of relationships to the end-of-life decision-making process, particularly family relationships.

summarizing key findings

PROTECTING SELF AND OTHERS

In my study, the older adult's motivation for completing an advance directive stemmed primarily from the following: 1) *protecting one's self* from the inappropriate use of life-sustaining technologies, overly zealous healthcare professionals, and pain and suffering at the end-of-life, and 2) *protecting others* from the burden of making difficult end-of-life decisions, paying for unnecessary expenditures, and feeling helpless. These older adults were hopeful the preparation of an advance directive would minimize conflict and promote positive relationships among family members, helping them to remain friends during and after the end-of-life decision-making process. Protecting children in this way is thought to protect family relationships for the future, a future that extends beyond the individual's death.

FACING ONE'S MORTALITY

Facing one's mortality was an integral aspect of preparing an advance directive for these older adults, and contributed to their ability to appreciate and live life to its fullest. Reflecting upon their own life and death was for most participants a positive and fulfilling (although not necessarily simple or painless) experience. Their approaches to death were forthright, practical, uplifting, and often amusing.

TALKING ABOUT DEATH

Talking about death was not always easy or comfortable, but it was an important component of preparing an advance directive for the participants. The conversations resulted in a perception of strengthened family relationships, sharing of values and beliefs about end-of-life, and a renewed valuing of life itself. Discussing death was emotionally charged at times for these older adults and the people they chose to talk to about their death.

CHOOSING AN ALLY

Choosing an ally (a spokesperson and advocate) was a complex undertaking that required a thoughtful assessment of persons within the participants' sphere of relations. They chose individuals with whom they had a close relationship, who were readily available, and whom they perceived to be level-headed and capable.

GETTING IT DONE

Completing an advance directive was a time-consuming and thought-provoking endeavour for many of the study participants. It required awareness, information, and careful contemplation. Completing an advance directive was not accomplished autonomously. Healthcare providers were conspicuously absent from most aspects of the process of completing a directive. The larger community, however, including the media, churches, and senior's centres played a role in raising awareness of advance directives and providing information.

All participants expressed satisfaction and a sense of accomplishment with completing their directives. I discovered that preparing an advance directive in many ways has more to do with living well than dying well. In the title of this book, *Living Will, Living Well*, I have reclaimed the term "living will" because it captures what is at the heart of the advance care planning process: living the best way a person knows how until death occurs.

messages for healthcare consumers

EXAMINE YOUR ATTITUDES AND BELIEFS ABOUT DEATH

Each participant spent time thinking about and articulating his or her own attitudes and beliefs about death and believed this was fundamental in the process of preparing an advance directive. Often this activity included contemplating the deaths of loved ones who had gone before them. For those who find this process difficult, turning to stories about death and dying in the literature may be helpful. Books such as *A Very Easy Death* (de Beauvoir, 1965), *W;t* (Edson, 1993), *A Ring of Endless Light* (L'Engle, 1980), *Tuesdays with Morrie* (Albom, 1997) and many others, all offer glimpses into the experience of death that may help in forming our own beliefs and attitudes.

BE INFORMED

Miguele de Cervantes, an author who lived in the sixteenth and seventeenth centuries, is credited with saying, "Forewarned, forearmed; to be prepared is half the victory." This quotation is relevant to those who wish to have some say in how their end-of-life unfolds. To prepare an advance directive adequately, one must have information about his or her health status, about life-sustaining options available, and about the expected consequences of using such interventions. The context for my study was the province of Alberta, Canada, and the legislative guidelines mentioned in this text are related to the *Personal Directives Act* published by the Province of Alberta in 1996. To learn more about legislative guidelines and requirements for preparing an advance directive in your province or jurisdiction, see the list of sources in Appendix C. Your provincial Office of the Public Guardian is also an excellent source of up-to-date information. Lawyers and healthcare providers may provide helpful consultation. Healthcare providers can provide guidance that is relevant and specific to your own health situation. Additional educational resources and advance directive templates that are readily available are listed in Appendix D.

ENGAGE YOUR HEALTHCARE PROVIDER(S) IN THE PROCESS

Most healthcare providers have demanding schedules, and a discussion about advance directives that focusses on future possibilities may not always be at the forefront of their consciousness. Although I suggest healthcare providers should initiate discussions about advance care planning, the current reality is it may be up to healthcare consumers to begin the dialogue. You may wish to ask questions about your own health status, the types of treatment you might be expected to receive at the end-of-life, and the likelihood of successful outcomes following their application. You may also want to discuss areas such as artificial nutrition and hydration and their relationship to comfort and suffering during the dying process.

IDENTIFY A SUBSTITUTE DECISION-MAKER

If a situation arises in which you are unable to make decisions for yourself, this role will be assigned to a substitute decision-maker.

In most jurisdictions, there is a mechanism by which you can appoint an individual(s) to fulfill this role. If you have not appointed an individual, your next-of-kin may be asked to make decisions on your behalf. In some jurisdictions, your next-of-kin will need to apply to be appointed as your substitute decision-maker. Under certain circumstances, the Office of the Public Guardian may become the substitute decision-maker. Appointing a substitute decision-maker in advance has many obvious benefits—it gives you control over who will be making decisions for you, you can ensure that this individual(s) is aware of your wishes, and it may allow decisions to be made in a timely and efficient manner.

TALK TO YOUR LOVED ONES

Arguably the most important aspect of preparing an advance directive (of even more significance than the completed document itself) is the discussion about your wishes with your loved ones, particularly the person(s) who will be acting as your substitute decision-maker(s). It is theoretically impossible and impractical to discuss every possible scenario that you might encounter at the end-of-life, but a discussion of your general values and the things that make your life worth living is essential. Is independence an important value for you? What about the ability to communicate with others? If resources were available, would you prefer to live at home or in a care facility? Under what kind of circumstances would you agree to a feeding tube, a respirator (breathing machine), or cardiopulmonary resuscitation? Engaging in a dialogue with your substitute decision-maker(s) about such questions will help them to understand your wishes. Such a discussion may also provide an opportunity to resolve any conflicts that might arise before a crisis occurs in which an expeditious decision must be made.

specific challenges for healthcare providers

One of the most striking findings of this study is the relative invisibility of healthcare providers throughout the older adult's process of completing an advance directive. In the following section, I suggest that healthcare providers should become more active participants in this process, and I propose a number of strategies for doing so. The strategies echo many of those identified for the healthcare consumer.

EXAMINE ONE'S OWN ATTITUDES AND BELIEFS ABOUT DEATH

In 1997, McKenzie made the following suggestion to physicians regarding advance directives: "The first practical advice would be 'physician know thyself.' I have a personal directive for myself and I review it every year...If you have not written a personal directive for yourself or assisted a close family member in doing so, you will discover some blind spots in terms of your personal biases" (p. 3).

Through conducting this research and in finally preparing my own advance directive, I learned that completing an advance directive is not necessarily a straightforward or simple task. Although not every healthcare provider may wish to prepare an advance directive, the findings of my study confirm that there are benefits to be gained for one's self and others from examining one's own attitudes and beliefs about death. Anderson (2001) restates this notion more emphatically indicating that healthcare professionals must "resolve their doubts [about death] to help patients resolve theirs" (p. 275). Shook (1992) concurs, stating that "the informed and knowledgeable professional has evaluated personal issues of life and death and feels comfortable and confident when informing patients and families about their rights" (pp. 34–35).

Study participants believed many of the healthcare professionals with whom they had come into contact perceived death to be the enemy. They also believed healthcare professionals, at times, had difficulty accepting the deaths of their patients. Without exception, participants shared traumatic stories about family members or friends who had suffered at the end-of-life, they believed, at the hands of healthcare professionals who had provided treatment that was of limited or no benefit, or even harmful. There is an urgent need for healthcare professionals to examine their own attitudes and beliefs about death and to consider reconceptualizing death as something other than the enemy. Healthcare professionals need to hold, in a delicate balance, both life and death as valuable outcomes. The findings suggest exploring one's own attitudes and beliefs about death may result in a greater appreciation of life.

BE INFORMED AND INVOLVED

As reported in the literature, and reaffirmed by participants in this study, the involvement of healthcare professionals in the completion of advance directives is limited. There is a general consensus by both healthcare providers and older adults that the input of healthcare professionals during the process of completing an advance directive can be both supportive and substantive. Participants in this study who had talked with a friend or family member who was also a health professional (most often a nurse) valued their knowledge and expertise. Health professionals are well-positioned and perhaps the most appropriate persons to provide this type of information.

RETHINK THE PURPOSE OF ADVANCE DIRECTIVES

Advance directives have been described as the solution to the problem of making decisions about life-sustaining treatment for incompetent patients (Singer, 1995). This description, however, fails to acknowledge the complexity of both "the problem" and "the solution." I agree with Singer (1995), who states that "advance care planning is not about legislation, lawyers, and doctors, but rather about relationships, communication, and families" (p. 9). For many participants in my study, there were no lawyers or doctors involved in the older adult's process of completing an advance directive, but references to relationships, communication, and the involvement of families were prevalent and considered of paramount importance. For the participants in this study, completing an advance directive was not just about making end-of-life treatment decisions in conditions of incapacity, it was about reflecting upon the existential questions of life and death.

In response to published studies reporting a relatively low completion rate of advance directives despite a number of different and often intensive programs designed to increase completion rates, Fins (1997) suggests that advance directives themselves are not to blame. He suggests that "shifting responsibility away from ourselves indicates our own denial of death and avoidance of much needed dialogue at the bedside of dying patients. It is too easy to scapegoat advance directives when it is clear that advance directives are going to be only as good as our efforts to obtain them [and use them]. Advance care planning will become effective only when we are more comfortable discussing end-of-life care and when we understand the cultural determinants that have made American medicine so hesitant to accept human finitude" (p. 520). One of the messages that I believe is implicit within Fins' response is that advance directives should not be conceptualized as a quick fix, an effortless solution to a well-defined problem. Rather, their development and implementation should be part of a consolidated and comprehensive approach to caring for patients at the end-of-life, one that takes time and reflection. Certainly for participants in this study, completing an advance directive was by and large a thoughtful process that unfolded over time, in some cases months and years.

MAKE ROOM FOR DISCUSSION OF DEATH
A number of studies have indicated that although older adults are willing participants in discussions about end-of-life and advance directives, they are hesitant to broach the subject with their healthcare providers. By introducing the subject of advance directives, healthcare professionals may legitimize the topic as one worthy of discussion. Individuals, including those in my study, often perceive that healthcare professionals are busy and do not have time to enter into such discussions about the future. Several participants in this study expressed appreciation for the opportunity to talk about their experience of preparing an advance directive. One participant near the end of our conversation stated, "When I read the piece of paper [the advertisement] that mentioned your exercise and what you were going to be investigating, I thought, 'What am I going to say?' I didn't think I'd have anything to say, and obviously your questions are bringing out deeper things." Heydemann (1997) suggests, "Personal directives allow us to converse about dying, to share our thoughts and feelings about death, and to take responsibility for very essential life/death decisions at a time when we are fully capable and in the midst of life itself...They will foster partnerships between family members and healthcare providers, so that we can walk more comfortably into the future" (p. 6).

Although this recommendation requires a time commitment from health professionals, there may be long-term gains to be made by engaging in such discussions sooner rather than later. Although difficult to measure, early and ongoing discussions may, in the end, actually save time and avoid conflict. If healthcare providers have an understanding of the values and beliefs of a patient, when the patient becomes incapable and unable to participate in the decision-making process, healthcare providers may not need to spend time finding and interviewing multiple family members and friends to determine the patient's desired level of care. Additionally, if a patient has clearly indicated for instance that she does not want to be given any chemotherapeutic agents in the context of terminal illness, it would not be necessary for healthcare professionals to undertake time-consuming research to establish the applicable chemotherapy treatment regime for her.

From my conversations with older adults in this study, it seems important for healthcare professionals to: 1) provide an opening for discussion of end-of-life issues, 2) communicate sensitively, 3) be at ease when talking about death, 4) be comfortable with emotion, 5) maintain a sense of humour, and 6) minimize the impact of ageist attitudes. For seniors who are alone and separated from their families, healthcare providers may be one of the few persons with whom they have regular contact. Healthcare professionals who are uncomfortable talking about death have a responsibility to seek out opportunities to develop their knowledge and skills in this area.

Although there are many reasons advance care planning ought to be encouraged, it cannot be required for ethical and legal reasons. One participant relayed the following anecdote about a friend: "When I was visiting Florida, a friend was going into the hospital and was made to sign a personal directive before he went in." Although the *Patient Self-Determination Act* (PSDA) in the United States requires healthcare organizations to ask patients whether or not they have an advance directive upon admission into their facilities, there is no requirement for individuals to complete one. This participant, however, perceived that non-completion of an advance directive was not an option for her friend. Did her friend feel coerced in any way? Is this an instance in which an individual complied so that he would not jeopardize subsequent care? Healthcare providers must balance the need to provide information about and encouragement of advance care planning without forcing individuals to make decisions that they are not ready or able to make.

FOSTER HEALTHCARE PROVIDER–PATIENT RELATIONSHIPS

When an individual presents an advance directive during hospital-ization, it may symbolize, a distrust of health providers and the healthcare system. Participants in this study expressed a concern that healthcare professionals have been socialized to act in a certain way to sustain life at all costs, whereas the participants generally preferred quality over quantity of life. Healthcare professionals need to be aware of the possibility that patients are wary of their motives, and they may need to work hard to re-establish a trusting provider-patient relationship. Open and sensitive communication is among the most effective tools for restoring and maintaining trust-ing relationships.

SUPPORT FAMILY INVOLVEMENT IN THE PROCESS

The importance of family members in the process of preparing an advance directive and in the role of agent or substitute decision-maker was central for study participants. Kuczewski (1996) suggests, "Interpreting our values usually involves the feedback of those close to us and often the advice of persons with professional expertise... If we assume that values do not simply emanate from some ineffable core within us but take shape through interaction with our environ-ment, the family is a natural part of this process" (p. 34). Studies have shown that "involving the family in the execution of the documents, while giving priority to the older person's preferences, alleviates the fears of future family conflicts" (Winland-Brown, 1998, p. 40). Healthcare professionals have a role to play in supporting family members through the process and encouraging intergenera-tional dialogue.

Although not directly addressed in this study, there is some evi-dence in the literature that substitute decision-makers may meet resistance in carrying out the wishes of their loved ones. Providing substitute decision-makers with additional information about nego-tiating the healthcare system might help to prevent some potential difficulties. Healthcare providers also have a responsibility to pro-vide substitute decision-makers with relevant information about their loved one's medical condition and treatment options, allow substitute decision-makers to share information about their loved ones with healthcare practitioners, and provide an environment that is supportive and free from coercion.

DEVELOP AND IMPLEMENT BEST END-OF-LIFE PRACTICES

In addition to supporting individuals and their families who enter into the process of completing an advance directive, healthcare professionals have an ethical responsibility to continue to improve end-of-life care in general. The major concerns around end-of-life care raised by study participants were the control of pain during the dying process and the appropriate use of life-sustaining technologies. Thoughtful practice and continued research into end-of-life care will help in the development of best practices.

apprehending death

In seeking a phrase that would capture the older adult's overall experience of preparing an advance directive, the one that I kept returning to was "apprehending death." To apprehend means to become cognizant of, to recognize, and to understand; it also means to anticipate, to imagine, and to fear (Oxford English Dictionary, 2002). Completing an advance directive requires first an awareness and recognition of the existence of advance directives and their purpose and potential. It demands that individuals project themselves into the future to imagine their own incompetency and death. For some, there is an undercurrent of fear—of pain, of the unknown.

Contrasted with the term "comprehend," which denotes embracing or understanding something in its entirety, "apprehend" denotes a clear understanding—but one that leaves some parts unknown (Oxford English Dictionary, 2002). We do not know, cannot know, and perhaps should not know what the death experience encompasses in its totality. Comprehension is impossible. Yet we can apprehend death's meaning to a certain extent. I feel that in completing this study, I am better prepared to contemplate my own death and to assist others as they prepare for theirs.

In recognition of the participants' contributions to shaping this study and its outcomes, and for their willingness to share their time and experiences, it seems only appropriate to give Alice the final word.

I've enjoyed sharing with you my experience of completing an advance directive. I've tried to present my story honestly and completely, to leave no stone unturned, nothing unsaid. I hope you will take some time to contemplate your own death and dying and examine the way you are living—maybe you'll even consider preparing your own advance directive! I hope you'll talk about death with your family and friends—they are the essence of what is truly important in life—not work, not money, not a bigger house. I hope that you will enjoy life to its fullest and experience all of its joys and few of its sorrows. And for me, I hope that when death knocks at my door, I will go gently into the night.

Reference List

Ackerman, T. F. (1997). Forsaking the spirit for the letter of law: Advance directives in nursing home [Editorial]. *Journal of the American Geriatrics Society, 45,* 114–116.

Ahronheim, J., & Weber, D. (1992). *Final passages: Positive choices for the dying and their loved ones.* New York: Simon & Schuster.

Albom, M. (1997). *Tuesdays with Morrie: An old man, a young man, and life's greatest lesson.* New York: Doubleday.

Anderson, M. (2001). *Sacred dying: Creating rituals for embracing the end of life.* Roseville, California: Prima Publishing.

Anderson, G. C., Walker, M. A. H., Pierce, P. M., & Mills, C. M. M. (1986). Living wills: Do nurses and physicians have them? *American Journal of Nursing, 86*(3), 271–275.

Backlar, P., & McFarland, B. (1996). A survey on use of advance directives for mental health treatment in Oregon. *Psychiatric Services, 47*(12), 1387–1389.

Barber, K. (Ed.) (2001). *The Canadian Oxford Dictionary.* Toronto: Oxford University Press Canada.

Beauchamp, T. L., & Childress, J. F. (1994). *Principles of biomedical ethics* (4th ed.). Oxford: Oxford University Press.

Bergum, V., & Dossetor, J. (2005). *Relational ethics: The full meaning of respect.* Hagerstown, Maryland: University Publishing Group.

Berrio, M. W., & Levesque, M. E. (1996). Advance directives: Most patients don't have one. Do yours? *American Journal of Nursing, 96* (8), 25–29.

Brookes, T. (1997). *Signs of life: A memoir of dying and discovery.* Toronto: Random House.

Browne, A., & Sullivan, B. (2006). Advance directives in Canada. *Cambridge Quarterly of Healthcare Ethics, 15,* 256–260.

Burgess, M. M. (1993). Intimate care for the dying: The need for a new social model. *Humane Medicine, 9*(1), 43–47.

Collins, L. G., Parks, S. M., & Winter, L. (2006). The state of advance care planning: One decade after SUPPORT. *American Journal of Hospice and Palliative Medicine, 23*(5), 378–384.

Colvin, E. R., Myhre, M. J., Welch, J., & Hammes, B. J. (1993). Moving beyond the Patient Self-Determination Act: Educating patients to be autonomous. *ANNA Journal, 20*(5), 564–568.

Coppola, K. M., Ditto, P. H., Danks, J. H., & Smucker, W. D. (2001). Accuracy of primary care and hospital-based physicians' predictions of elderly outpatients' treatment preferences with and without advance directives. *Archives of Internal Medicine, 161,* 431–440.

Crable, C. H. (2005, April 5). Schiavo ordeal prompts increase in living wills. *Kansas State Collegian* [online]. Retrieved February 22, 2007, from http://classstation.spub.ksu.edu/Collegian/article.php?a=5625

de Beauvoir, S. (1965). *A very easy death.* P. O'Brian (Trans.). New York: Pantheon Books. (Original work published 1964)

Degrazia, D. (1999). Advance directives, dementia, and 'the someone else problem.' *Bioethics, 13*(5), 373–391.

de Raeve, L. (1993). Informed consent and living wills. *European Journal of Cancer Care, 2,* 150–156.

Ditto, P. H., Danks, J. H., Smucker, W. D., Bookwala, J., Coppola, K. M., Dresser, R., Fagerlin, A., Gready, M., Houts, R. M., Lockhart, L. K., & Zyzanski, S. (2001). Advance directives as acts of communication: A randomized controlled trial. *Archives of Internal Medicine, 161,* 421–430.

Dooley, J., & Marsden, C. (1994). Healthcare ethics forum '94: Advance directives: The critical challenges. *AACN, 5*(3), 340–345.

Doukas, D. J., & McCullough, L. B. (1991). The values history: The evaluation of patient's values and advance directives. *The Journal of Family Practice, 32*(2), 145–149.

Downie, J. (1992). Where there is a will, there may be a better way: Legislating advance directives. *Health Law in Canada, 12*(3), 73–80.

Edson, M. (1993). *W;t.* New York: Faber and Faber.

Emanuel, L. L. (1995). Reexamining death: The asymptotic model and a bounded zone definition. *Hastings Center Report, 25*(4), 27–35.

Emanuel, L. L., & Emanuel, E. (1989). The medical directive: A new comprehensive advance care document. *Journal of the American Medical Association, 261*(22), 3288–3293.

Enright, D. J. (Ed.). (1983). *The Oxford book of death.* Oxford: Oxford University Press.

Fins, J. J. (1997). Advance directives and SUPPORT. *Journal of the American Geriatrics Society, 45,* 519–520.

Fisher, R., Ross, M. M., & MacLean, M. J. (Eds.). (2000). *A guide to end-of-life care for seniors.* Ottawa: Health Canada.

Fitzgerald, M. (1994). Adults' anticipation of the loss of their parents. *Qualitative Health Research, 4*(4), 463–479.

Freeborne, N., Lynn, J., & Desbiens, N. A. (2000). Insights about dying from the SUPPORT project. *Journal of the American Geriatrics Society, 48*(3), S199-S205.

Gadamer, H. G. (1982). *Truth and method.* New York: Crossroad.

Gaines, E. J. (1993). *A lesson before dying.* New York: Vintage Books.

Gamble, E. R., McDonald, P. J., & Lichstein, P. R. (1991). Knowledge, attitudes and behavior of elderly persons regarding living wills. *Archives of Internal Medicine, 151,* 277–280.

Glover, Charles (composer). (1864). *Finigan's wake: The popular Irish song.* New York: William A. Pond & Company.

Griffin, M. (1993). Caring for those who choose to die at home. *Humane Medicine, 9*(1), 38–42.

Hamel, C. F., Guse, L. W., Hawranik, P. G., & Bond, J. B. (2002). Advance directives and community-dwelling older adults. *Western Journal of Nursing Research, 24*(2), 143–158.

Hansot, E. (1996). A letter from a patient's daughter [on being a patient]. *Annals of Internal Medicine, 125,* 149–151.

Hardingham, L. B. (1997). Ethics in the workplace. Personal directives: Part II. Implications for Caregivers. *AARN Newsletter, 53*(2), 14–15.

Hatfield, R., & McHutchion, E. (1993). A dialogue on care of the dying. *Humane Medicine, 9*(1), 27–33.

Hayley, D. C., Cassel, C. K., Snyder, L., & Rudberg, M. A. (1996). Ethical and legal issues in nursing home care. *Archives of Internal Medicine, 156*(3), 249–256.

Heffner, J. E., Fahy, B., & Barbieri, C. (1996). Advance directive education during pulmonary rehabilitation. *Chest, 109*(2), 373–379.

Heydemann, R. (1997). A spiritual perspective of personal directives. *Health Ethics Today, 5*(1), 5–6.

Higgins, G. L. (1993). Discovering a patient's values for advance directives. *Humane Medicine, 9*(1), 52–56.

High, D. M. (1993a). Advance directives and the elderly: A study of intervention strategies to increase use. *Gerontologist, 33*(3), 342–349.

High, D. M. (1993b). Why are elderly people not using advance directives? *Journal of Aging and Health, 5*(4), 497–515.

Ho, V. W. K., Thiel, E. C., Rubin, H. R., Singer, P. A. (2000). The effect of advance care planning on completion of advance directives and patient satisfaction in people with HIV/AIDS. *AIDS Care, 12*(1), 97–108.

Hoffman, D. E., Zimmerman, S. I., & Tompkins, C. (1997). How close is enough? Family relationships and attitudes toward advance directives and life-sustaining treatments. *Journal of Ethics, Law, and Aging, 3*(1), 5–24.

Institute of Medical Ethics Working Party on the Ethics of Prolonging Life and Assisting Death. (1993). Advance directives: Partnership and practicalities. *British Journal of General Practice, 43*, 169–171.

Johns, J. L. (1996). Advance directives and opportunities for nurses. *IMAGE: Journal of Nursing Scholarship, 28*(2), 149–153.

Karel, M. J., Moye, J., Bank, A., & Azar, A. R. (2007). Three methods of assessing values for advance care planning: Comparing persons with and without dementia. *Journal of Aging and Health, 19*(1), 123–151.

Kavanagh, R. E. (1972). *Facing Death*. Middlesex, England: Penguin Books.

Kelley, K. (1995). The Patient Self-Determination Act: A matter of life and death. *Physician Assistant, 19*(3), 49, 53–56, 59–60.

Kilner, J. F. (1990). *Ethical criteria in patient selection: Who lives? Who dies?* New Haven: Yale University Press.

Kollas, C. D., & Boyer-Kollas, B. (2006). Closing the Schiavo case: An analysis of legal reasoning. *Journal of Palliative Medicine, 9*(5), 1145–1163.

Kowalski, N. C. (1986). Anticipating the death of an elderly parent. In T. A. Rando (Ed.), *Loss and anticipatory grief* (pp. 176–199). Lexington, Massachusetts: Lexington Books.

Kuczewski, M. G. (1996). Reconceiving the family: The process of consent in medical decision-making. *Hastings Center Report, 26*(2), 30–37.

Kuhse, H. (1999). Some reflections on the problem of advance directives, personhood, and personal identity. *Kennedy Institute of Ethics Journal, 9*(4), 347–364.

L'Engle, M. (1980). *A ring of endless light*. New York: Farar, Straus, Giroux.

Leslie, N. S., & Badzek, L. A. (1996). Patient utilization of advance directives in a tertiary hospital setting. *Journal of Nursing Law, 3* (2), 23–33.

Levenson, J. L., & Pettrey, L. (1994). Controversial decisions regarding treatment and DNR: An algorithmic guide for the uncertain in decision-making ethics. *American Journal of Critical Care, 3*(2), 87–91.

Lo, B. (1995). Improving end of life care: Why is it so hard? *Journal of the American Medical Association, 274*(20), 1634–1636.

Matzo, M. L. (1997). The search to end suffering: A historical perspective. *Journal of Gerontological Nursing, 23*(3), 11–17.

May, T. (1997). Reassessing the reliability of advance directives. *Cambridge Quarterly of Healthcare Ethics, 6*, 325–338.

McKenzie, K. R. (1997). Personal directives and reality: A physician's perspective. *Health Ethics Today, 5*(1), 2–4.

Mendelssohn, D. C., & Singer, P. A. (1994). Advance directives in dialysis. *Advances in Renal Replacement Therapy, 1*(3), 240–250.

Molloy, D. W., Guyatt, G., Alemayehu, E., & McIlroy, W. E. (1991). Treatment preferences, attitudes toward advance directives and concerns about health care. *Humane Medicine, 7*(4), 285–290.

Molloy, D. W., Guyatt, G. H., Russo, R., Goeree, R., O'Brien, B. J., Bédard, M., Willan, A., Watson, J., Patterson, C., Harrison, C., Standish, T., Strang, D., Darzins, P. J., Smith, S., & Dubois, S. (2000). Systematic implementation of an advance directive program in nursing homes: A randomized controlled trial. *Journal of the American Medical Association, 283*(11), 1437–1444.

Murray, S. A., Sheikh, A., & Thomas, K. (2006). Advance care planning in primary care. *British Medical Journal, 333*(7574), 868–869.

Neumark, D. E. (1994). Providing information about advance directives to patients in ambulatory care and their families. *Oncology Nursing Forum, 21*(4), 771–773.

Nicolasora, N., Pannala, R., Mountantonakis, S., Shanmugam, B., DeGierolamo, A., Amoateng-Adjepong, Y., & Manthous, C. A. (2006). If asked, hospitalized patients will choose whether to receive life-sustaining therapies. *Journal of Hospital Medicine, 1* (3), 161–167.

Ott, B. B. (1999). Advance directives: The emerging body of research. *American Journal of Critical Care, 8*(1), 514–519.

Oxford English Dictionary [Online]. (2002). Available: http://dictionary. oed.com

Pearlman, R. A. (1996). Challenges facing physicians and healthcare institutions caring for patients with mental incapacity. *Journal of the American Geriatrics Society, 44,* 994–996.

Perrin, K. O. (1997). Giving voice to the wishes of elders for end-of-life care. *Journal of Gerontological Nursing, 23*(3), 18–27, 50–56.

Prendergast, T. J. (2001). Advance care planning: Pitfalls, progress, promise. *Critical Care Medicine, 29*(2), N34-N39.

Province of Alberta. (1996). *Personal Directives Act: Chapter P-4.03.* Edmonton, Alberta: Queen's Printer.

Remen, R. N. (1996). *Kitchen table wisdom: Stories that heal.* New York: Riverhead Books.

Ross, P., & West, D. J. (1995). Advance directives: The price of life. *Nursing Economics, 13*(6), 355–361.

Sam, M., & Singer, P. A. (1993). Canadian outpatients and advance directives: Poor knowledge and little experience but positive attitudes. *Canadian Medical Association Journal, 148*(9), 1497–1502.

Sanderson, C. D. (1995). Educating the community on advance directives. *Tennessee Nurse, 58*(2), 23.

Sansone, P., & Phillips, M. (1995). Advance directives for elderly people: Worthwhile cause or wasted effort? *Social Work, 40*(3), 397–401.

Sarton, M. (1973). *As we are now.* New York: Norton & Company.

Sawchuck, P. G., & Ross Kerr, J. (2000). Choices, decisions, and control: Older adults and advance care directives. *Canadian Nurse, 96*(7), 16–20.

Scott-Maxwell, F. (1968). *The measure of my days.* New York: Penguin.

Shaw-MacKinnon, M. (2001). Birth, death and the Eleusinian mysteries. In C. Shields & M. Anderson (Eds.), *Dropped threads: What we aren't told* (pp. 220–229). Toronto: Vintage Canada.

Shook, M. (1992). Health decisions: Maintaining control of health care choices. *Nurse Practitioner Forum, 3*(1), 30–34.

Shore, A. D., Rubin, H. R., Haisfield, M. E., McGuire, D. B., Zabora, J. R., & Krumm, S. (1993). Health care providers' and cancer patients' preferences regarding disclosure of information about advance directives. *Journal of Psychosocial Oncology, 11*(4), 39–53.

Singer, P. (1995). Advance directive fallacies. *Health Law in Canada, 16*(1), 5–9.

Sonnenblick, M., Friedlander, Y., & Steinberg, A. (1993). Dissociation between the wishes of terminally ill parents and decisions by their offspring. *Journal of the American Geriatrics Society, 41,* 599–604.

Teno, J. M., Licks, S., Lynn, J., Wenger, N., Connors, A. F., Phillips, R. S., O'Connor, M. A., Murphy, D. P., Fulkerson, W. J., Desbiens, N., & Knaus, W. A. (1997). Do advance directives provide instructions that direct care? *Journal of the American Geriatrics Society, 45,* 508–512.

Teno, J., Lynn, J., Connors, A. F., Wenger, N., Phillips, R. S., Alzola, C., Murphy, D. P., Desbiens, N., & Knaus, W. A. (1997). The illusion of end-of-life resource savings with advance directives. *Journal of the American Geriatrics Society, 45,* 513–518.

Thorevska, N., Tilluckdharry, L., Tickoo, S., Havasi, A., Amoateng-Adjepong, Y., & Manthous, C. A. (2005). Patients' understanding of advance directives and cardiopulmonary resuscitation. *Journal of Critical Care, 20,* 26–34.

Tonelli, M. R. (1996). Pulling the plug on living wills: A critical analysis of advance directives. *Chest, 110*(3), 816–822.

Webster's II New Riverside Dictionary. (1984). New York: Berkley Books.

Winland-Brown, J. E. (1998). Death, denial, and defeat: Older patients and advance directives. *Advanced Practice Nursing Quarterly, 4*(2), 36–40.

Winters, G., Glass, E., & Sakurai, C. (1993). Ethical issues in oncology nursing practice: An overview of topics and strategies. *Oncology Nursing Forum, 20*(10), 21–34.

Wood, L. C., & DelPapa, L. A. (1996). Nurses' attitudes, ethical reasons, and knowledge of the law concerning advance directives. *IMAGE: Journal of Nursing Scholarship, 28*(4), 371.

Yamani, M., Fleming, C., Brensilver, J. M., & Brandstetter, R. D. (1995). Using advance directives effectively in the intensive care unit. *The Journal of Critical Illness, 10*(7), 465–473

Appendix A

Guiding Interview Questions

1. How did you come to decide to complete a directive?
2. What were your reasons for completing a directive?
3. How did you prepare to complete the directive?
   a. What information did you gather?
   b. Who did you talk to?
   c. Who did you involve in the process?
   d. How did he or she react/respond to being involved?
   e. Did you have any concerns about completing a directive?
4. How did you decide what to include in your directive?
   a. What were some of your decisions?
   b. What did these decisions mean to you?
   c. Do you have any concern that you may change your mind (that your decisions now might not be the ones you would want if you were incapacitated)?
   d. Do you have any concern that your wishes might not be respected?
5. Did you select a person(s) to be your healthcare agent?
   a. How did you come to a decision about who would be your agent?
   b. What criteria did you use?
   c. What do you see as the qualities or characteristics necessary to be a good agent?
   d. How did you discuss your decision with your agent?
   e. How did the person(s) respond?
   f. What questions did the person(s) have?

g. Do you have any concern that the person(s) you selected would not be able to follow through with his/her commitment to you (that he or she would not be able to follow through with your decisions)?

6. What was the process of completing a directive like for you? What thoughts ran through your mind?
   a. How was this process similar to or different from completing an estate will?

7. Did completing your directive make you think about your own mortality?
   a. What does it mean to you to die well?
   b. What does a good death look like?
   c. How would you describe your own beliefs about death and dying?

8. Are there any other aspects of preparing a directive that you would like to talk about?

Appendix B

Sample Advance Directive[1]

1. **APPOINTMENT OF HEALTHCARE AGENT**

   I, _____ , appoint _____ as my agent to make decisions on my behalf.

2. **COMING INTO EFFECT**

   This directive will have effect only when I lack capacity to make a decision about any personal matter, and I will lack capacity when my agent signs a written declaration to that effect after consulting with a physician or a psychologist who has completed a declaration as required by the regulations in the *Personal Directives Act*.

3. **AGENT'S POWERS**

   I give my agent powers to make all decisions relating to the following:

   a) my healthcare, including providing consent, accepting or refusing any or all medical care;

   b) where I am able to reside and with whom I am able to live and associate;

   c) what social and recreational activities I am to engage in; and

   d) generally, all day-to-day matters, including decisions respecting nutrition, hygiene, clothing, and safety.

   I have discussed my values and beliefs with my agent and trust in his/her ability to make a decision that I would be comfortable with.

---

1. Adapted from study participants' directives (reflects Alberta legislative requirements).

4. PERSONAL DECISIONS

My agent must instruct my healthcare service providers based on the following guidelines:

4.1. I do not wish my life to be prolonged by artificial means when I am in a coma or a persistent vegetative state and, in the opinion of my physician and other consultants, have no known hope of regaining awareness and higher mental functions, no matter what is done.

4.2. In the event of a mild stroke or mild dementia, I want all major treatments such as CPR, life-saving surgery, or antibiotics to continue, but would want a ventilator, dialysis, or tube feeding on a short-term basis only.

4.3. I wish to be kept comfortable and free from pain. This means that I may be given pain medication even though it may dull consciousness and indirectly shorten my life.

4.4. If I am unable to care for myself, I do not wish my family to be burdened with my care. I wish to be cared for in a private or publicly-funded facility.

4.5. I have signed an organ donor card and authorize my agent to inform my caregivers of this to hasten the process of organ harvesting after my death.

5. ACCESS TO DOCUMENTS AND INFORMATION

I authorize and permit my agent to access all confidential documents to which I am entitled personally including, but not limited to, full access to my medical records, Revenue Canada records, any safety deposit boxes I may have, as well as all personal financial information.

6. OTHER

In the event that my instructions in this personal directive are ambiguous or insufficient, I direct my agent as follows:

a) to make the decision that my agent believes I would make in the circumstances, given my agent's knowledge of my wishes, beliefs, and values; and

b) if my agent does not know what decision I would make, to make the decision my agent believes is in my best interest in the circumstances.

This directive is made after careful contemplation. I hope you who care for me will feel morally bound to follow its mandate. I recognize that this appears to place a heavy responsibility upon you, but this directive is made with the intention of relieving you of such responsibility and placing it upon myself in accordance with my strong convictions.

DATED, SIGNED, AND WITNESSED
I make this personal directive on the 1st day of *month, year,* at *city/town, province.*

Signed: _____

Witness: _____

Date: _____

Appendix C

Legislative Guidelines

Here is a list of websites and phone numbers to help you access the legislative guidelines related to advance directives (instructional and/or proxy directives) in Canada.

With the exception of Nunavut, there is legislation concerning advance directives for healthcare in all provinces and territories within Canada. There is no Canadian federal legislation governing advance care planning.

It is important to ensure that an advance directive is made in compliance with local legislation. Although there is no legislation concerning reciprocity across provinces, most provinces and territories will generally accept an advance directive from another jurisdiction if it complies with the law in the jurisdiction where it will be used. Even in jurisdictions where advance directives are not recognized legal documents, they do carry moral weight and healthcare professionals, based on their codes of ethics, should respect an individual's previously expressed capable wishes.

Further information can be obtained from the Office of the Public Guardian in each region. The phone number for the Office of the Public Guardian is listed in the government pages of most phone books.

ALBERTA

The *Personal Directives Act* is available:
- online at www.qp.gov.ab.ca/documents/Acts/P06.cfm?frm_isbn=0779721837

- from the Queen's Printer by phone in Edmonton: (780) 427–4952; or toll-free within the province of Alberta at dial 310–0000 followed by the above phone number

BRITISH COLUMBIA
The *Representation Agreement Act* is available:
- online at www.qp.gov.bc.ca/statreg/stat/R/96405_01.htm
- by phone at (250) 387–3309

MANITOBA
The *Health Care Directives Act* is available:
- online at web2.gov.mb.ca/laws/statutes/ccsm/h027e.php
- by phone in Winnipeg and outside Manitoba at (204) 945–3101, or toll-free in Manitoba at 1–800–321–1203

NEW BRUNSWICK
The *Infirm Persons Act* is available:
- online at www.gnb.ca/0062/acts/acts/i-08.htm
- by phone through the Office of the Attorney General at (506) 453–3132

NEWFOUNDLAND
The *Advance Health Care Directives Act* is available:
- online at www.assembly.nl.ca/legislation/sr/statutes/a04_1.htm
- by phone at (709) 729–3604

NORTHWEST TERRITORIES
The *Personal Directives Act* is available:
- online at www.justice.gov.nt.ca/PDF/ACTS/Personal_Directives.pdf
- by phone at (867) 920–6418

NOVA SCOTIA
The *Medical Consent Act* is available:
- online at www.gov.ns.ca/legislature/legc/statutes/medcons.htm
- by phone at (902) 424–8941

NUNAVUT

Nunavut does not have legislation concerning advance directives for healthcare.

ONTARIO

The *Substitute Decisions Act* is available:
- online at www.e-laws.gov.on.ca/html/statutes/english/elaws_statutes_92s30_e.htm
- by phone at (416) 326–5300, or toll-free at 1–800–668–9938

PRINCE EDWARD ISLAND

The *Consent to Treatment and Health Care Directives Act* is available:
- online at www.gov.pe.ca/law/statutes/pdf/c-17_2.pdf
- by phone (902) 368–4000

QUEBEC

The *Quebec Civil Code (Book 5, Chapter 9, c. 64, s. 2130–2185 (1991))* is available:
- online at www2.publicationsduquebec.gouv.qc.ca/dynamicSearch/telecharge.php?type=2&file=/CCQ_/CCQ_A.html
- by phone at (418) 643–5150, or toll-free in Quebec at 1–800–463–2100

SASKATCHEWAN

The *Health Care Directives and Substitute Health Care Decision Makers Act* is available:
- online at www.qp.gov.sk.ca/documents/English/Statutes/Statutes/H0-001.pdf
- by phone at (306) 787–6894, or toll-free at 1–800–226–7302

YUKON

The *Care Consent Act* is available:
- online at www.gov.yk.ca/legislation/acts/Bcaco.pdf
- by phone at (867) 667–8573, or toll-free in Yukon at 1–800–661–0408

Appendix D

Educational Resources

The following is a list of educational resources related to advance directives. It includes materials that I have found to be readable and informative.

AGING WITH DIGNITY
P.O. Box 1661
Tallahassee, FL 32302–1661
Phone: (888) 5WISHES (594–7437)
Website: www.agingwithdignity.org
    An advance directive document entitled "Five Wishes," and accompanying video instructional material, is available through this organization for a charge. A copy of the "Five Wishes" document can be viewed on the website for no charge.

CENTER FOR PRACTICAL BIOETHICS
Harzfeld Building
1111 Main Street, Suite 500
Kansas City, MO 64105–2116
Phone: (816) 221–1100, or toll-free 1–800–344–3829
Website: www.practicalbioethics.org
    An advance directive workbook entitled *Caring Conversations* is available online, free of charge, in English and Spanish.

DALHOUSIE END OF LIFE PROJECT

Health Law Institute, Dalhousie University
6061 University Avenue
Halifax, NS B3H 4H9
Phone: (902) 494–6881
Website: as01.ucis.dal.ca/dhli/cmp_welcome/default.cfm
   The website includes a section on advance directives.

DYING WITH DIGNITY

55 Eglinton Avenue East, Suite 802
Toronto, ON M4P 1G8
Phone: (416) 486–3998, or toll-free 1–800–495–6156
Website: www.dyingwithdignity.ca
   One of the mandates of this charitable society is to provide infor-
   mation about advance directives. Advance directive templates
   and other information about dying with dignity are included with
   membership in the society.

GOVERNMENT OF MANITOBA

Phone: (in Winnipeg and outside Manitoba) (204) 945–3101
Phone: (toll-free in Manitoba) 1–800–321–1203
Website: www.gov.mb.ca/health/livingwill.html
   The website contains information about Manitoba's *Health Care Dir-
   ectives Act* and a link to the province's Health Care Directive form.

JOINT CENTRE FOR BIOETHICS, UNIVERSITY OF TORONTO

88 College Street
Toronto, ON M5G 1L4
Phone: (416) 978–2709
Website: www.utoronto.ca/jcb/outreach/living_wills.htm
   The website has living will forms available for downloading in
   English, French, and Italian. Some of the forms are specific to
   several health conditions (such as HIV, cancer). An instructional
   video is available for a charge.

MINISTRY OF THE ATTORNEY GENERAL (ONTARIO)

Website: www.attorneygeneral.jus.gov.on.ca/english/family/pgt/
poakit.asp

Phone: (416) 326–2200, toll-free 1–800–518–7901

The website has links to a number of resources, such as power
of attorney kits and answers to frequently asked questions. For
Ontarians, *A Guide to the Substitute Decisions Act* is available online.

NEWGRANGE PRESS CANADA INC.

86 Ferrie Street West

Hamilton, ON L8L 1C9

Phone: (905) 529–8922

Website: www.newgrangepress.com/let_me_decide_series_books_
videos.html

This publisher sells a series of booklets and videos entitled *Let Me
Decide*, which were created by Dr. D. W. Molloy, Hamilton Civic
Hospital, and others to assist individuals in making choices about
their future healthcare wishes. The booklets are available in a
number of languages.

OFFICE OF THE PUBLIC GUARDIAN, ALBERTA

Phone: (in Edmonton and outside Alberta) (780) 427–0017

Phone: (toll-free in Alberta) dial 310–0000 then ask for (780) 427–0017

Website: www.seniors.gov.ab.ca/services_resources/opg/persdir/
publications/index.asp

The Office of the Public Guardian has produced a series of materials
called *Choosing Now for the Future* for individuals wishing more
information about personal directives. Free copies are available
online in English, French, Chinese, German, Punjabi, and Spanish.

ONTARIO SENIORS' SECRETARIAT

777 Bay Street, Suite 601C

Toronto, ON M7A 2J4

Phone: toll-free 1–888–910–1999

Website: www.culture.gov.on.ca/seniors/english/programs/
advancedcare/

An easy to read *Advance Care Planning Guide* is available. The booklet
includes contact information for a number of other organizations.

OTTAWA HEALTH RESEARCH INSTITUTE

725 Parkdale Avenue

Ottawa, ON K1Y 4E9

Phone: (613) 761–4395

Website: decisionaid.ohri.ca/decaids.html

The Ottawa Health Research Institute has compiled a list of
decision-making aids on a variety of healthcare topics, including
end-of-life decisions such as tube-feeding placement, use
of mechanical ventilation in individuals with severe chronic
pulmonary disease, and admission to a care facility.

PROVINCIAL HEALTH ETHICS NETWORK

#507 Guardian Building

10240—124 Street

Edmonton, AB T5N 3W6

Phone: (780) 447–1180, or toll-free 1–800–472–4066

Website: www.phen.ab.ca/perdir/

This informative website includes the booklet called *Preserving
Dignity: Personal Directives*, links to other resources, information on how to write a personal directive, and a number of
sample directives.

YUKON HEALTH AND SOCIAL SERVICES

Website: www.hss.gov.yk.ca/programs/decision_making/care_
consent_act/advance_directives/

Phone: (867) 667–3673, or toll-free 1–800–661–0408

This site includes a number of brochures and information booklets related to advance care directives and the role of substitute
decision-makers.

Index

advance care planning, 8, 109, 122–23
advance directives
    agent's role in, 72, 82–83, 104, 108
    barriers to, 10–12, 39, 56
    becoming aware of, 16, 17–21
    benefits of, 9–10, 12, 25–26, 110,
      112, 118
    children's role in, 66–67, 72, 110
    components of, 23–24, 103–04
    definition, 6, 7
    and establishing health status,
      100–03
    examples of having and not
      having one, 2–4
    failure of strategies for
      completing, 116–17, 122
    family consultation on, 22–23,
      67–68, 71–73, 120
    feeling of security from,
      109–13, 118
    friends' role in, 72, 77–78, 99, 124
    getting information on, 21–22,
      23–24, 25–26, 96, 97, 119
    health professionals as consul-
      tants on, 73–74, 100–02, 121–23
    health professionals' attitudes
      about, 36–37, 83–84, 122–23
    history of, 8–9

    information sources for, 21–22,
      97–99, 147–50
    interview questions for, 137–38
    and issue of trust, 91–93
    legal requirements for, 7–8, 105,
      109, 124
    legislative guidelines for, 97–98,
      119, 143–45
    list of resources for, 147–50
    personal statements in, 109, 111
    preparation of, 23–24, 25, 33–34,
      38, 62, 72, 73
    preparing alone, 78–80, 91–92
    and protecting others, 30, 31,
      37–38, 77–78, 88, 89–90, 117
    as protection from health
      system, 34–36
    reasons for completing, 117–18
    reflection on, 110–13, 117
    samples of, 105–06, 139–41
    simplicity of, 107–08
    sources of information for,
      21–22, 97–99, 147–50
    specificity of, 11, 107–08
    templates for, 105–06, 139–41
    writing, 96–97, 98, 99, 103–08,
      110. *See also* agents/substitute
      decision-makers; death

and dying; families; health
  professionals; life-
  sustaining treatment
agents/substitute decision-makers
  children as, 86–88, 91, 92
  choosing, 82–83, 86–91, 118,
    119–20
  description of, 24–25
  friends as, 83, 89–90
  health professionals as, 85, 89, 90
  and issue of trust, 91–93
  and legalities, 88–89
  resources on, 147–50
  role as patient advocate, 82–83, 84
  role in advance directives, 72,
    82–83, 104, 108
  spouses as, 88
  working with health profes-
    sionals, 84, 86, 125–26
aging, 47–48, 49, 56, 62
Albom, Mitch, 31–32
allies, 25
Anderson, Megory, 1, 57, 107, 121
artificial nutrition, 32, 119

birth, 27–28, 49, 65
body donation, 101, 103
Brookes, T., 46–47
Burgess, M. M., 56–57
Buturlin, Alexander S., 53

cardiopulmonary resuscitation,
  2–3, 101, 106, 107. See also life-
  sustaining treatment
ceremony and death, 57, 66, 70
Cervantes, Miguel de, 119
children
  as agents, 86–88, 91, 92
  and death of parents, 74–78
  experience of death, 59, 66

guilt over burdening them, 30,
  104, 112, 117
hiding death from, 46, 57–58
as motivation for advance
  directives, 31, 33–34, 37–38,
  89–90
and preparation of advance
  directives, 66–67, 72, 110
and quality of life, 51
talking about death with, 69–72.
  See also family
church, 21, 98, 99
communication and quality of life,
  38, 40–41, 120
contemplation. See reflection
costs, 35–36, 109
CPR (cardiopulmonary
  resuscitation), 2–3, 101, 106,
  107. See also life-sustaining
  treatment
cremation, 66

death and dying
  acceptance of, 10, 51–53, 54–57,
    60, 61–62, 62, 127
  attitude towards effected by life
    experience, 54–55, 60–62
  ceremony and, 57, 66, 107
  and children, 46, 57–58, 59, 66,
    69–72, 74–78
  comprehending a family
    member's, 74–78
  comprehending one's own, 10,
    44–47, 48, 61, 62, 75, 126
  conceptions of, 22, 23, 48–50, 55
  conceptions of life after death,
    47, 50, 51, 52–53, 54, 56–57
  connection with birth, 27–28,
    49, 65
  with dignity, 28–29, 34, 60, 104,
    147, 148, 150

distancing ourselves from, 31,
    50, 55, 57, 59–60, 78
and dividing possessions, 74
experience of, 2–5, 29–30, 32, 66
fear of, 51–52, 53–54, 55–56, 58, 62
health professionals' attitude
    towards, 57, 58, 121
at home, 106–07
humour and, 52, 55, 66, 69–71,
    74, 117
imagining how one dies, 50–51,
    101, 106–07
language used to describe, 59–60
literature on, 118
and pain, 27–28, 32
portrayals in media, 57, 58–59
reflection on, 63, 95, 118, 127
resistance to idea of, 74–78
rituals for, 57, 66, 107
scepticism about lack of fear of,
    55–56
and symbols, 68
as taboo topic, 57–60, 74–75, 77
talking about as fear reducer,
    53, 55, 70
talking about as preparation for
    advance directives, 66, 69–70,
    74–75, 76–78, 117, 123
talking about with family, 66,
    69–70, 74–75, 76–78, 117
talking about with friends,
    77–78, 89
de Beauvoir, Simone
    as agent, 84
    on death, 31, 49–50, 65
    on dying, 81
    on fear of death, 53
    on view of parent's death by
        child, 15, 77
dignity, dying with, 28–29, 34, 60,
    104, 147, 148, 150

doctors. *See* health professionals
donations, organ and body, 101–03

emotion
    as barrier to thinking about
        death, 68, 69, 77
    and preparing advance
        directives, 99, 100, 104
end-of-life decision-making
    awareness of, 16, 17–22
    example of absent, 3, 26
    example of effective, 3–5
    guilt from, 9–10, 30, 32–33, 34
    and money, 24, 74. *See also*
        advance directives
estate wills, 111

family
    and choosing an agent, 86
    as component of quality of life,
        41, 127
    and discussions of organ
        donation, 102–03
    and health professionals, 125
    involved in preparation of
        advance directives, 22–23,
        67–68, 71–73, 120
    as motivation for advance
        directives, 19–20, 30, 37–38
    specific instructions for, in
        advance directives, 105
    talking about death with, 66,
        69–70, 74–75, 76–78, 117
fear
    alleviation of, by advance
        directives, 111
    of being buried, 53
    of causing guilt, 30
    of changing one's mind, 10–11
    of death, 51–52, 53–54, 55–56, 58,
        62, 70

of dying, 22, 29
of loss of personal connection, 36
of pain, 29, 126
of parent's death, 76
feeding tubes, 18, 36–37, 107. *See also*
life-sustaining treatment
Fins, J. J., 122, 123
Fitzgerald, M., 76
Freud, Sigmund, 54
friends
and advance directives, 72,
77–78, 99, 124
as agents, 83, 89–90
and quality of life, 127
funerals, 48

Gadamer, H. G., 50
Gaines, E. J., 54
government legislation, 97–98, 119,
143–45
grief, 77
guilt
of children over their parents,
76, 84
easing of, by making end-of-life
decisions, 9–10, 30, 32–33, 34
over decisions on life-sustaining
treatment, 30–31, 32, 89–90
of parents over burdening
children, 30, 104, 112, 117

Hansot, Elisabeth, 58, 84
Hatfield and McHutchion, 58
Hazlitt, William, 54
health professionals
as agents, 85, 89, 90
attitude towards death, 57, 58, 121
behaviours necessary for end-of-
life consultation, 124–26
busyness of, 102, 123

conflicted attitude towards
advance directives, 36–37,
83–84, 122–23
and individuality of patients, 28,
34, 39–40, 46, 81
overtreatment by, 29–30, 34–36
and pain control, 27
and power struggle with
patients, 84–86, 125
questions on their role in dying
process, 33, 41–42, 74, 80
relations with patient's family,
125
role in helping with advance
directives, 20–22, 73–74, 78,
79, 89–90, 100–02, 103, 119,
121–23
strategies for best practices,
120–26
use of life-sustaining treatment,
2–3, 35–37, 83–84
view of quality of life, 58, 85–86,
125
working with agents, 84, 86,
125–26
helplessness, 28, 31–32, 58
Heydemann, R., 123
Higgins, G. L., 63
hospitals. *See* health professionals;
life-sustaining treatment
humour and death, 52, 55, 66, 69–71,
74, 117
hydration, 32, 101, 119

immortality, 53–54

Kavanagh, R. E., 56, 58–59, 60, 76–77,
95, 111
Kierkegaard, Søren A., 56
kitchen tables, discussions at,
68–69

Kowalski, N.C., 76
Kuczewski, M.G., 72–73, 125

lawyers
    and choosing an agent, 86, 90
    as consultants on advance
        directives, 19, 98, 99, 100
    role in writing advance
        directives, 105, 108–09
legalities, 7–8, 88–89, 105, 109, 124
life-sustaining treatment
    agent's ability to deal with, 83, 90
    costs of, 35–36
    difficulty of decisions over, 25,
        32–33, 55–56, 106–07
    guilt over decisions on, 30–31,
        32, 89–90
    and health professional's use of,
        2–3, 35–37, 83–84
    power struggle over, 84–86
    provisions for, in advance
        directives, 67–68, 99, 100–01,
        107–08, 119, 120, 124
    Quinlan and Schiavo cases, 18–19
    resources on, 147–50
    templates for, in advance
        directives, 105–06
living wills, 7–8, 118

McKenzie, K.R., 121
media, 18–19, 57, 58–59
medical intervention. See life-
    sustaining treatment
money and advance care planning,
    8, 24, 74, 109

nurses/nursing
    author's experience as, 2–3, 39
    and helping with advance direc-
    tives, 20–21, 73, 78, 79, 89–90, 101.
    See also health professionals

obituaries, 70
Office of the Public Guardian,
    99–100, 119, 120, 143, 149
organ donation, 101, 102–03, 106, 108

pain
    fear of, 29, 126
    as motivation, 26–28
    noted in advance directives, 106,
        107, 119
    while dying, 27–28, 32
palliative care, 3–4, 41
Patient Self-Determination Act (PSDA)
    (US), 124
Perrin, K.O., 73
personal autonomy, 9, 38–39, 111
personal directives, 7. See also
    advance directives
Personal Directives Act (Alberta),
    97–98, 119, 143, 144
philosophy
    of death, 22, 47, 49–50, 52–53,
        56–57
    and existential questions, 63
    of life, 61–62, 127
    of personhood, 38–40
    and preparation of advanced
        directive, 10, 22–23, 38, 73. See
        also quality of life; values
proxy directives, 6, 11

quality of life
    effect on attitude towards death,
        60–62
    health professionals attitude
        towards, 58, 85–86, 125
    what qualifies as, 38, 39, 40–41,
        51, 120, 127. See also
    philosophy; values
Quinlan, Karen Ann, 18

reflection
    on advance directives, 110–13, 117
    on life and death, 63, 95, 118, 127
religious convictions, 49, 52, 53, 54, 105
religious organizations, 21, 98, 99
Remen, R. N., 68–69
respirator support. *See* life-sustaining treatment
resuscitation, 2–3, 101, 106, 107. *See also* life-sustaining treatment
retirement planning, 111
Rousseau, Jean-Jacques, 55

Sansone and Phillips, 87
Sarton, May, 63
Schiavo, Terri, 18–19
Scott-Maxwell, Florence, 27–28, 52–53, 55, 89
Shook, M., 121
Singer, P., 103, 122
Spark, Muriel, 51

storytelling, 68–69, 72–73
substitute decision-makers, 119–20, 125–26, 147–50. *See also* agents/substitute decision-makers
suicide, 53
symbols, 68

technology, 35–37, 52, 99. *See also* life-sustaining treatment
television, 59
treatment directives, 6, 7

values
    deciding on one's, 38, 60, 68, 72–73
    statement of, in advance directives, 104, 105, 109, 120. *See also* philosophy; quality of life

wakes, 70
Winland-Brown, J. E., 56